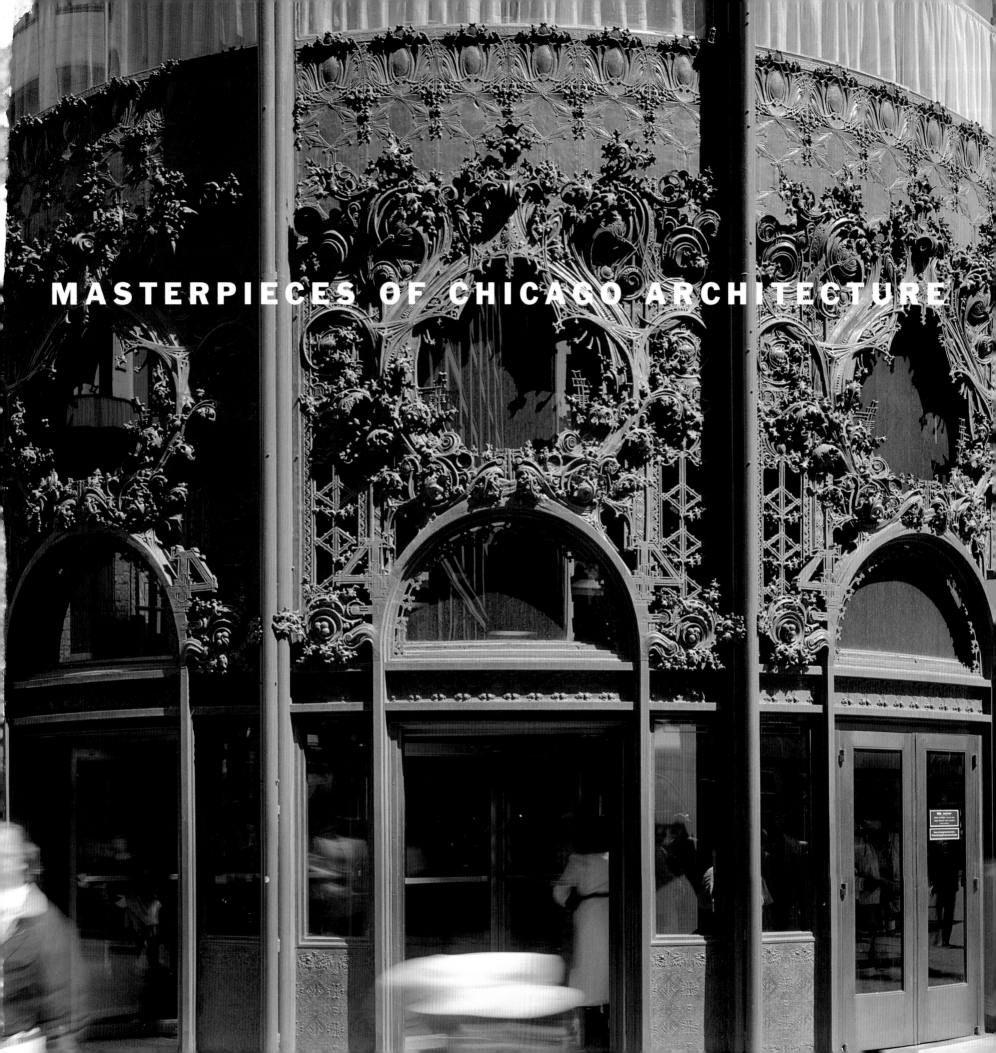

MASTERPIECES OF CHICAGO ARCHITECTURE

CHICAGO ARCHITECTURE

John Zukowsky and Martha Thorne

Preface by Stanley Tigerman

RIZZOLI
NEW YORK

THE ART INSTITUTE OF CHICAGO

First published in the United States of America in 2004 by
Rizzoli International Publications, Inc.
300 Park Avenue South, New York, NY 10010

ISBN: 0-8478-2596-5
LCCN: 2003115866

Page 1: Schlesinger and Mayer Store (see page 46)
Pages 2–3: Buckingham Fountain (see page 78)
Pages 28–29: Head House, Chicago Municipal Pier (see page 60)

This book is a publication of the Ernest R. Graham Study Center
for Architectural Drawings at The Art Institute of Chicago.

Designed by Abigail Sturges
Edited by Elizabeth Johnson
Photo edited by Annie Feldmeier
Printed and bound in China

2005 2006 2007 2008 / 10 9 8 7 6 5 4 3 2

CONTENTS

8 **PREFACE**
Stanley Tigerman

10 Introduction
EXHIBITIONS AND OBSERVATIONS
ON BLUEPRINTS, BRICKS, AND MORTAR
John Zukowsky

28 **MASTERPIECES OF CHICAGO**
ARCHITECTURE:
BUILDINGS AND DRAWINGS

30 Stewart-Bentley Building
Peter B. Wight for Carter, Drake & Wight

31 Lenox Building
Peter B. Wight for Carter, Drake & Wight

32 Rookery Building
Burnham and Root

36 Fine Arts Building
John Wellborn Root for Burnham and Root

38 Exhibition Pavilion
Charles Atwood for D.H. Burnham and Company

39 Reliance Building
Charles Atwood for D.H. Burnham and Company

40 Fisher Building
Peter J. Weber for D.H. Burnham and Company

44 Trading Room of the Chicago Stock Exchange
Louis H. Sullivan for Adler and Sullivan

Detail from the Fisher Building (see page 43).

46 Schlesinger and Mayer Store
Louis H. Sullivan

48 *A System of Architectural Ornament*
Louis H. Sullivan

48 McVickers Theatre
Louis H. Sullivan

49 Krause Music Store
Louis H. Sullivan

50 Fuller ("Flatiron") Building
Frederick P. Dinkelberg for Daniel H. Burnham and Company

52 *The Plan of Chicago*
Daniel H. Burnham and Edward H. Bennett

56 Rock Crest/Rock Glen
Walter Burley Griffin and Marion Mahony Griffin

58 Avery Coonley Playhouse
Frank Lloyd Wright

60 Head House, Chicago Municipal Pier
Charles Sumner Frost

62 3400 North Sheridan Road
Peter J. Weber for White and Weber

64 Chicago Tribune Tower Competition

66 Chicago Tribune Tower
Howells and Hood

68 London Guarantee and Accident Building
Alfred S. Alschuler

72 Palmer House
Holabird and Roche

76 Boulevard Apartments
Dubin and Eisenberg

78 Buckingham Fountain
Bennett, Parsons, Thomas & Frost

80 1500 Lake Shore Drive
James Edwin Quinn for McNally and Quinn

82 Carbide and Carbon Building
*Daniel Burnham Jr. and Hubert Burnham for
D.H. Burnham and Co. (The Burnham Brothers)*

84 North West Tower
Perkins, Chatten & Hammond

86 Field Building
*Alfred Shaw for Graham, Anderson,
Probst & White*

88 The Attic Club
David Adler, Architect

90 Dymaxion Car
R. Buckminster Fuller

92 Travel and Transport Building
*Edward H. Bennett, John Holabird,
and Hubert Burnham*

96 Proposed Tower of Water and Light
Ralph Walker for Voorhees, Gmelin & Walker

98 Mrs. Kersey Coats Reed House
David Adler, Architect

NORTHWESTERN MEMORIAL HOSPITAL
100 Montgomery Ward Memorial Building
James Gamble Rogers

102 Wesley Memorial Hospital
Thielbar and Fugard

104 Herbert A. Jacobs House
Frank Lloyd Wright

Detail from the Schlesinger and Mayer
Store (see page 46).

106 Highways of the Future
Hugh Ferriss

106 Bridge over Caldwell Avenue
James Edwin Quinn

106 Congress Street Expressway
James Edwin Quinn

108 Illinois Institute of Technology
Ludwig Mies van der Rohe

112 860–880 Lake Shore Drive
Ludwig Mies van der Rohe

116 Ruth Ford House
Bruce Goff

118 O'Hare International Airport
Ralph Burke Associates

122 Inland Steel Building
*Walter Netsch and Bruce Graham for
Skidmore, Owings & Merrill*

124 Marina City
Bertrand Goldberg Associates

126 Chicago Civic Center
Jacques Brownson for C.F. Murphy Associates

130 Time-Life Building
Harry Weese and Associates

132 Seventeenth Church of Christ Scientist
Harry Weese and Associates

134 Abraham Lincoln Oasis, Tri-State Tollway
David Haid & Associates

136 First National Bank Building
C.F. Murphy Associates with Perkins & Will

138 McCormick Place
Gene Summers for C.F. Murphy Associates

140 John Hancock Center
*Bruce Graham and Fazlur Khan for
Skidmore, Owings & Merrill*

142 Water Tower Place
*Loebl Schlossman Bennett & Dart with C.F. Murphy
Associates*

144 The Titanic
Stanley Tigerman

146 Illinois Regional Library for the Blind
and Physically Handicapped
Stanley Tigerman & Associates

148 Late Entries to the Chicago Tribune Tower
Competition

150 McDonald's Floating Restaurant
SITE (Sculpture in the Environment, Inc.)

152 Painted Apartment
Krueck & Olsen Architects

154 Chicago Board of Trade
Helmut Jahn for C.F. Murphy Associates

156 One South Wacker Drive
Helmut Jahn for C.F. Murphy Associates

158 James R. Thompson Center
Helmut Jahn for C.F. Murphy Associates

162 Chicago and Northwestern Terminal Building
Helmut Jahn for C.F. Murphy Associates

164 United Airlines Terminal One
Murphy/Jahn Architects

168 190 South LaSalle Street
John Burgee Architects with Philip Johnson

172 NBC Tower
Adrian Smith for Skidmore, Owings & Merrill

174 Morton International Building
Ralph Johnson for Perkins & Will

176 American Medical Association
Kenzo Tange

178 Crate and Barrel Store
Solomon Cordwell Buenz & Associates, Inc.

178 Crate and Barrel Headquarters
Ralph Johnson for Perkins & Will

180 Greyhound/Trailways Bus Terminal
Nagle Hartray & Associates

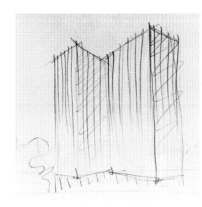

Perspective sketch of high rise buldings
by Mies van der Rohe (see page 112).

182 International Terminal
Ralph Johnson for Perkins & Will

186 Little Village Academy
Carol Ross Barney for Ross Barney + Jankowski Architects

190 House in Lincoln Park
Tadao Ando

194 Markow Residence
Douglas Garofalo for Garofalo Architects

196 Blue Cross/Blue Shield of Illinois
James Goettsch for Lohan Associates

198 Adler Planetarium and Astronomical Museum
Expansion
Dirk Lohan for Lohan Associates

200 Lincoln Park Zoo Main Store and Rooftop Café
Joe Valerio for Valerio Dewalt Train

204 North Avenue Beach House
Dan Wheeler for Wheeler Kearns Architects

208 St. Patrick's Roman Catholic Church Renovation
Laurence Booth for Booth Hansen Associates

210 Hotel Sofitel
Jean-Paul Viguier

212 New Terminal at Midway Airport
Steven Reiss for HNTB Architecture

216 Chinese American Service Center
Jeanne Gang for Studio Gang/O'Donnell

218 Epilogue
CHICAGO IN THE NEW MILLENNIUM
Martha Thorne

235 Appendices
LIST OF EXHIBITIONS AND THEIR DESIGNERS

236 **COMMITTEE ON ARCHITECTURE 2003**

237 **ACKNOWLEDGMENTS**

238 **INDEX**

240 **PHOTOGRAPHY CREDITS**

PREFACE

STANLEY TIGERMAN

Chicago, 2003

Chicago's architectural community has had the good fortune of enjoying more than two decades of respectability from the Art Institute of Chicago's Architecture Department headed by the John Bryan Curator of Architecture John Zukowsky. Zukowsky was ably assisted in the early years by Associate Curator Pauline Saliga and, more recently, by Associate Curator Martha Thorne. There has been a staggering plethora of delightful exhibitions supplemented by catalogues, books, lectures, docent-led tours, by far the largest architectural oral history archive of any museum, and perhaps most importantly, unprecedented grants from the National Endowment for the Arts and the National Endowment for the Humanities as well as significant corporate financial support. The selection compiled here is culled from the department's sizable archives, but is more, however, than just another feather in this department's already overstuffed cap.

The examples shown here are not merely a chronological history, but a typological survey as well. Chicago's architects are not simply unthinking practitioners whose work is informed by technique; many are theoretically speculative as well. For every Jacques Brownson who built well, there was a Reginald Malcolmson who dreamed about the future. For every seminal modernist like Mies van der Rohe, there was an equal and opposite unreconstituted classicist like Daniel Burnham. And while the conventional view of Chicago's contributions to world architectural history has often been portrayed as one-dimensionally oriented toward structural expression, this book shows that multivalence was always alive and well in Chicago.

While it is true that this is, after all, Chicago in all its architecturally splendiferous history—what other American city could boast the many buildings by Louis Sullivan, Frank Lloyd Wright, Mies van der Rohe, and the several Chicago schools populated by lesser luminaries (Root, Keck, et al.)? — the particular way in which the Institute's curators have instilled their own brand of inclusivist good will shines through in this important publication.

This is not, however, simply a litany of examples of Chicago's well-earned place in the architectural firmament of the past, but it is about a promising future as well. In contradistinction to those who would diminish Chicago's architectural present, the book includes the work of Brininstool/Lynch, Dirk Denison, Doug Garofalo, Jeannie Gang, Ralph Johnson, Ron Krueck, Pete Landon, Margaret McCurry, Eva Maddox, Andrew Metter, Ben Nicholson, Rick Phillips, Katherine Quinn, John Ronan, Elva Rubio, Chris Rudolph, Linda Searl, Joe Valerio, and David Woodhouse. Such a roster points to a promising future that continues Chicago's architecture and design primacy apace.

The above-mentioned designers are held out here as both descendants and forebears of a multidimensionalism that has always characterized the best of Chicago's architects. For example, two major points of view—the rear guard and the avant-garde—are represented here: the first with Landon, McCurry, Phillips, Quinn, Rudolph, and Searl; the second with Brininstool/ Lynch, Denison, Johnson, Krueck, Maddox, Metter, Rubio, Woodhouse, Garofalo, Gang, Nicholson, Ronan, and Valerio. Similarly, a difference in focus on the built environment or on theory is worth noting: the first with Brininstool/Lynch, Johnson, Landon, McCurry, Metter, Phillips, Quinn, Rubio, Rudolph, Searl, and Woodhouse; the second with Denison, Garofalo, Gang, Krueck, Maddox, Nicholson, Ronan, and Valerio.

Though many more individuals and firms are doing superb work in Chicago, even this list suggests the Architecture Department's openness to and inclusive optimism about the ongoing architectural scene. I wish especially to single out John Zukowsky and his well-known penchant for inclusivity. Having been closely associated with many of the department's exhibition installations (and by extension, having an in-depth relationship with the Architecture Department's chief curator), I am in somewhat of a unique position of observing (through participation) his passion for and belief in Chicago architecture. The architectural archive has been dramatically increased by his powers of persuasion, as well as his broadly based selection of architects and designers for the department's installations. The nexus of his many efforts have induced a palpable energy to the world of Chicago architecture.

All of this energy has positioned the Art Institute's Architecture Department clearly as the most significant operation of its kind in the United States and, if I may be so bold, the world. This book carries the entire tradition one important step further by pausing, if only for a moment, to present these characteristic examples of the Architecture Department's seminally important collection.

Enjoy!

LEFT

LUDWIG MIES VAN DER ROHE

Illinois Institute of Technology, Crown Hall.

EXHIBITIONS AND OBSERVATIONS ON BLUEPRINTS, BRICKS, AND MORTAR

JOHN ZUKOWSKY

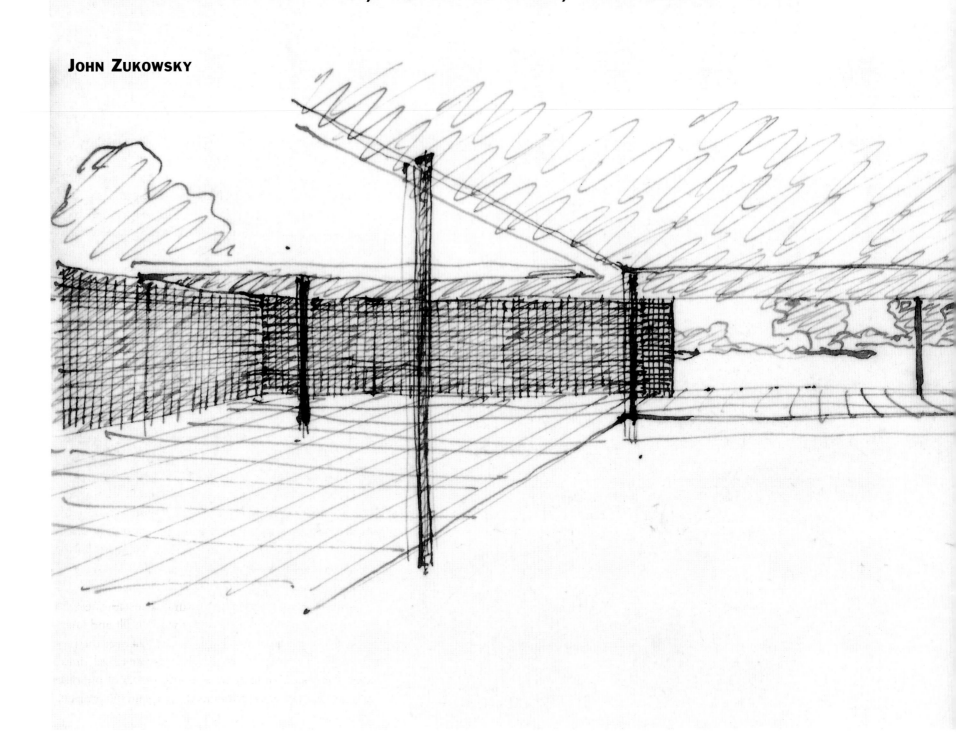

Chicago! The popular images that people have had of this city range from gangsters of the 1920s controlling the city streets, to Carl Sandburg's famous description of Chicago's stockyards as "hog butcher to the world." Yet, perhaps more than most American cities, Chicago is linked, in the minds of many residents and visitors, to architecture. What local taxi driver doesn't know about the city's tallest skyscrapers such as the Hancock and Sears Towers, or even somewhat smaller ones such as Marina City? Some of those same urban ambassadors, along with a number of other city residents, can also tell you about the likes of Louis Sullivan, Frank Lloyd Wright, and Mies van der Rohe. Architects today such as the current partners of Skidmore, Owings & Merrill, Helmut Jahn, and Stanley Tigerman have joined the city's celebrity list, though perhaps not quite at the level of Oprah Winfrey, Michael Jordan, and Sammy Sosa. What other city could boast an army of hundreds of volunteer docents such as those from the Chicago Architecture Foundation, all of whom eagerly provide regularly scheduled tours of the city's great buildings? I find it difficult to believe that architects and architecture can figure so prominently in the public consciousness of other American, Asian, or European cities.

With this popular architectural consciousness in mind, this volume will look at the work, built and imagined, of some of Chicago's great architects over the past century, with an emphasis on their architectural drawings. We shall illuminate those masterpieces of building and design in brief descriptions that explain the projects' importance.

FIG. 2

FRANZ LIPP

Perspective study for a proposed Forest Chapel, del. Lee Marzolf, ca. 1928. Charcoal pencil on board. Gift of Franz Lipp through the Chicago Botanic Garden.

Our survey will show that creativity in design is not just a thing of the past in Chicago. The range of monuments that readers will encounter spans the decades from the early Chicago School skyscrapers of architects such as Burnham & Root and Sullivan, to the famed Prairie School works of Frank Lloyd Wright and his followers, through the influential minimally modernist masterworks by Mies van der Rohe and his disciples, to more recent contextual designs by the so-called postmodern architects here, the Chicago Seven, which includes Stanley Tigerman and Helmut Jahn. Beyond that impressive history, architects today such as Douglas Garofalo and Jeanne Gang are among those Chicagoans who have taken up the banner for continuing the dynamic reputation that Chicago has always had for architecture.

The book concludes with an assessment of the latest works by Chicago's up-and-coming architects. All of the architectural drawings and archival treasures published here come from the permanent collections of the Department of Architecture at the Art Institute of Chicago, a collection that developed in relation to the architectural history of the city.

In the past I have traced the story of the Art Institute's collection of architectural drawings back to 1919, when architect Peter B. Wight (1838–1925) gave his scrapbook of striking watercolors and presentation drawings (see p. 30) to the museum's famous Burnham Library of Architecture so that students at the School of the Art Institute could consult it. Many more treasures came to the library over the next six decades, including much material by Louis Sullivan (1856–1924), which in good part came from George Grant Elmslie, the executor of Sullivan's estate. Perhaps even historically more important was Sullivan's striking *System of Architectural Ornament* (see p. 48), which the Art Institute and some of his friends commissioned him to create shortly before his death. Additionally, significant collections of work by Daniel H. Burnham (1846–1912), John Wellborn Root (1850–1891), Walter Burley Griffin (1876–1937), and his wife Marion Mahony (1871–1962) came to the library.

When I began work in the Art Institute's library in 1978 as the Architectural Archivist, I was instructed to organize a series of changing exhibitions in the library's architectural gallery to make the public and architectural professionals alike aware of the rich heritage housed within the Art Institute's walls, and to expand the collection itself to incorporate the archives of less-well-known architects and contemporary designers. It was then that, with the active encouragement of Head Librarian Daphne Roloff, I organized an exhibition called *The Plan of Chicago: 1909–1979*, which showcased the recently restored drawings for that famous plan created by Daniel H. Burnham and Edward H. Bennett (see p. 52).

In order to expand the holdings, I contacted the heirs of Chicago's famous architects, many of whom had also become practitioners. I often tell the story that in the pre-Internet era of the 1970s all one had to do was look up "Architects" in the Yellow Pages and many recognizable names, perhaps a generation or two removed from the original, jumped out. By doing this we were gifted, for example, a wealth of material on Alfred Alschuler (1876–1940); Richard Yoshihiro Mine (1894–1981), Chicago's first Japanese-American designer (see p. 64); and the collection of sketches by Ludwig Mies van der Rohe (1886–1969), which was given to us by A. James

Speyer, the museum's Curator of Twentieth-Century Art and one of Mies's early students (Fig. 1; also see p. 109).

Because of the library's increased activity in both exhibiting and acquiring architectural artwork and, in part, the outcome of an institution-wide self-study in 1981, the newly appointed director of the museum, James N. Wood, recommended to the Art Institute's Board of Trustees that a curatorial Department of Architecture be created. The Trustees agreed, and the library's collection of architectural drawings was combined with the architectural fragments—decorative pieces, large and small, from demolished or altered Chicago buildings—within the American Arts department to create this new department. As with the other curatorial departments at the Art Institute, an advisory committee was established. Museum trustee David Hilliard served as its chair, and its members included developers, architects, and architectural aficionados (see appendix of the Committee on Architecture). At the time of its creation, noted architect Robert A.M. Stern gave a speech at the Art Institute that was published soon after in *Inland Architect* (July–August 1982). In it, he outlined his hopes for the department in a five-year plan that encompassed thorough historic exhibitions on Chicago architecture in relation to its interactions with other cities, and its impact on other environments. He

FIG. 3

RICHARD TEN EYCK ASSOCIATES

Perspective study of a Cessna 337 Float Plane, January 12, 1967. Colored pencil and pastel on paper. Gift of Richard Ten Eyck.

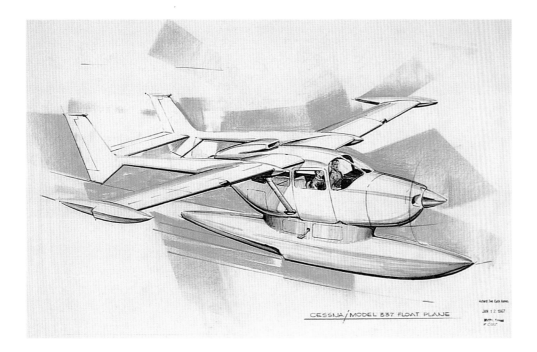

suggested that we "examine the impact of Chicago architecture and thereby what Chicago architecture is or was on its own. Full dress. Bring out all the documents; bring out all the photographs—whatever it takes to *really* show it." He furthered stated, "Your institution here is young; this new department, it's wiry. It's only got one or two people to fight it out in a nasty little room in the basement, and that's where things are going to happen." Over the more than twenty years since the establishment of the department and that speech, the department's architectural exhibition, collecting, and research activities have grown to the point where the department has made its impact on the architectural scene in Chicago and the United States, and, in so doing, has gone through several major changes, architecturally and programmatically. In a way, things did indeed "happen."

The department continued to expand its acquisitions through the generosity of architects and their heirs to include a wealth of more contemporary works, including major architectural collections by Paul Schweikher, William Deknatel, Ludwig Hilberseimer, Bruce Goff, Bertrand Goldberg, Stanley Tigerman, and Helmut Jahn. In preparation for a book and exhibition for the twentieth-anniversary celebration of the Pritzker Architecture Prize (1999), Associate Curator Martha Thorne, with the help of Cindy and Jay Pritzker, led a concerted effort to acquire representative drawings by the award winners, adding substantial pieces to our department's collection (see p. 190). And, as an extension of the department's collecting policies, we initiated in 1983, under the leadership of volunteer Betty Blum, the Chicago Architects Oral History project with the taping of Paul Schweikher's reminiscences. From then until the end of 2002, with funding from a variety of public and private sources, we amassed more than seventy oral histories of architects—a collection unique in the United States if not the world. Through the efforts of Ms. Blum, colleague Annemarie van Roessel, and others, the transcripts of those interviews, an incredible resource on the history of Chicago architecture, are available on the Art Institute's website. As a refinement of its collecting and exhibitions policy, the department, through the funding of the National Endowment for the Arts and the efforts of then Associate Curator Pauline Saliga, expanded its scope to include industrial, graphic, and landscape design. This expanded definition of archi-

tectural art enabled us to collect important works by landscape architects Franz Lipp and Gertrude Kuh as well as industrial designers John Polivka and Richard Ten Eyck (Figs. 2, 3). In keeping with this broadening of our interests, and to support young architects, in 1988 retired building contractor Harold Schiff established the Schiff Foundation Fellowship. This major annual award is given to an advanced undergraduate or graduate architectural student in Chicago. The fellowship winners donate their entry portfolios to the department's permanent collection, and so far the collection includes the works of more than fifteen up-and-coming designers. Further support from Harold Schiff and the Graham Foundation for Advanced Studies in the Fine Arts allowed the department to hire Kristine Fallon, FAIA, and her staff in 2003 to help us determine what to collect in terms of electronic data on architecture.

With all these acquisitions, the permanent collection had grown to over 130,000 drawings and several hundred building fragments and architectural models, and needed a new home. Stanley Tigerman designed the Ernest R. Graham Study Center for Architectural Drawings, funded by the Graham Foundation for Advanced Studies in the Fine Arts. Opened in 1991, it consists of 3,000 square feet of remodeled space within the Art Institute's original structure. The Graham Center provided space for storage of the collection, public access to those documents via appointment, and office space for the staff. Tigerman designed it so that a number of our drawings, models, and fragments could be featured within a dramatic framework similar to an exhibition (Fig. 4). The new space was a great improvement, but our architectural drawings collections had continued to increase, and within a decade the Graham Study Center was overcrowded.

Thanks to the help of the Conservation and Operations staff at the Art Institute, we were awarded a major grant from the National Endowment for the Humanities (NEH) to remodel one floor of a warehouse near the University of Illinois into museum-quality storage for all of our architectural drawing, model, and fragment collections. This project was undertaken in 2001–2002 by the design-build firm of McClier, and it more than tripled our storage space, giving the architecture collection growing room for at least another decade. (As before, researchers can consult this collection by appointment.) Our depart-

FIG. 4

STANLEY TIGERMAN

The Ernest R. Graham Study Center for Architectural Drawings, 1991.

ment's long-time Technical Specialist Luigi Mumford, who retired in 2002, coordinated this move with the assistance of Kate Butterly (now our Collections Manager) and Jennifer Brand.

Even before these new homes were constructed for the collection, we had been given a small permanent exhibition space for our architectural fragments. As part of a 1985 renovation of the original Art Institute building led by Adrian Smith (of Skidmore, Owings & Merrill), John Vinci designed the space atop the museum's famous central entry staircase. The permanent exhibition project, entitled *Fragments of Chicago's Past*, was installed by then Associate Curator Pauline Saliga who also augmented that first installation with additional fragments in 1990.

With the establishment of a curatorial department came a need to create a support team to organize programs—lectures, tours, and events—that would relate to the department's activities. The Architecture Society, formed in 1982 with James N. Alexander as its first president, was renamed the Architecture and Design Society in 1993. They are perhaps best known over the past two decades and more for organizing public lectures of such superstar architects as Tadao Ando, Santiago Calatrava, Michael Graves, Rem Koolhaas, Kisho Kurokawa, Fumihiko Maki, and Richard Meier, and design stars such as thinker Larry Keeley, Dieter Rams of Braun, Andree Putmann, and Martin Thaler of IDEO.

Publications form an important part of the public face of the Architecture Department. Since its creation, our department has produced a number of major books that have had both general and scholarly appeal. Titles such as *Mies Reconsidered* (1986), *Chicago Architecture: 1872–1922* (1987), *Chicago Architecture and Design: 1923–1993* (1993), *Louis H. Sullivan: A System of Architectural Ornament* (1990), and *Building for Air Travel: Architecture and Design for Commercial Aviation* (1996) have won awards and received praise from critics and scholars alike. Other titles have been equally well received and range from international contemporary subjects such as *Austrian Architecture and Design* (1991), *Building in a New Spain* (1992), *Japan 2000* (1997), *The Pritzker Architecture Prize* (1999), and *Skyscrapers: The New Millennium* (2000) through transportation design studies such as *2001: Building for Space Travel* (2001) and *Modern Trains and Splendid Stations* (2002). Along with those major publications the department also initiated a series of inexpensive exhibition booklets called Architecture in Context that document varied subjects such as *The Postwar American Dream* (1985), *Paul Rudolph* (1987), *The Modern Movement* (1988), *Louis Kahn in the Midwest* (1989), *Stanley Tigerman: Recent Projects* (1989), and *Moscow Avant-Garde Architecture* (1991). A great strength of the publications program is that the books are, more often than not, team efforts that bring together a variety of academics and practitioners who provide intellectually rich essays. In all, our publications in the field of architectural studies prompted one reviewer to observe, in the *Journal of the Society of Architectural Historians* (June 1991), that our museum "has the most productive department of architecture of any museum in the nation."

Our exhibitions have not gone unnoticed either. A number of them have won design awards from the Chicago Chapter of the American Institute of Architects for their installations and have been positively received by the press. As with our books, our exhibitions are often shaped not by one person but by a democratic team, usually convened in a series of brainstorming meetings or planning sessions that determine the themes and content of the exhibits and their adjunct programs. Our exhibition installations themselves have become the major trademark of our work in the Department of Architecture. That is because they attempt to remind all of our visitors that architecture is the creation and manipulation of space, and that the space itself is as much a part of the exhibition as the objects within the gallery. In many ways, this is akin to having a conceptual artist create a gallery installation, but at the Art Institute we have commissioned a wide variety of architects, local and international, to install the exhibitions as thematic frameworks for the objects on display (see Appendix for a chronological list of exhibitions and their designers). Thus, the installation architect becomes a critical member of our multifaceted team. The spectacular installations organized by Martin and Mildred Friedman at the Walker Art Center in Minneapolis during the 1980s—particularly *Tokyo Form and Spirit* (1986), which had rooms designed by different Japanese architects—inspired us to do these types of exhibition designs. Realizing that an architectural installation could help to make the subject come alive for the visitor, I decided to

FIG. 5

STANLEY TIGERMAN

Entrance to *Chicago Architecture: 1872–1922*, installed at the Art Institute of Chicago, July 16 through September 5, 1988.

do something like that for our 1988 showing of *Chicago Architecture: 1872–1922*.

The Art Institute showed *Chicago Architecture* almost a year after it had opened the temporary exhibitions gallery at the Musée d'Orsay in Paris in 1987 and had traveled to the Deutsches Architekturmuseum in Frankfurt. Because it had been seen in Europe, I felt it was important that this large exhibition be presented to the Chicago public in a new light. I chose Stanley Tigerman to design the installation because of his interest in Chicago's architectural history. He was one of the curators of the famous *Chicago Architects* exhibit in 1976 during the nation's bicentennial, as well as the 1980 exhibition at the Museum of Contemporary Art on *Late Entries to the Chicago Tribune Tower Competition*. We had also seen Tigerman's other installation designs such as the Thonet showroom at the Merchandise Mart (1981), *The Great American Cemetery* (1981) done with artist Richard Haas, and the *Garden of Eden* niche (1984) at the Deutsches Architekturmuseum. With major support from the NEH, we were able to construct Tigerman's spectacular series of exhibition rooms. The exhibition focused on the period of Chicago architecture from the Great Fire of 1871 to the Chicago Tribune Tower competition of 1922, with Europe's influence on Chicago and then Chicago's and America's influence on the world through the creation of the Chicago School of commercial building and the Prairie Style of residential design. Visitors to the show walked through classically detailed spaces that incorporated specially made models, including one that showed much of the city in ruins after the catastrophic fire of 1871 (Fig. 5). At the end, the museum store included specially designed book displays for the great historic figures of Chicago architecture—Burnham, Sullivan, and Wright. These kiosks echoed the large exhibition spaces dedicated to each of those three heroic designers that were in the second half of the show (Fig. 6).

The installation was a great success with the press and general public alike, attracting over 135,000 visitors. It demonstrated that an active architectural installation could indeed work well with the objects on display without overshadowing their importance. In fact, many lamented that this was not a permanent installation. When we planned a sequel to that exhibition called *Chicago Architecture and Design: 1923–1993* (funded by

the NEH with substantial support from the Continental Bank), we again enlisted Tigerman to coordinate. He approached it as a world's fair of Chicago architecture, a series of theme corridors designed by eight mid-career Chicago architects. Upon entering the space, one walked back and forth through history in a series of time tunnels, tracing the impact of each particular building and design type between 1923 and 1993. Tigerman created each space to look as if it were still under construction, showing the metal stud walls underneath what the younger architects designed within. In the order of their presentation in the show: Howard Decker designed the space for Planning the region; Steven Wierzbowski, Transportation; Maria Whiteman, Government and Institutions; Kathryn Quinn, Commercial structures; Ronald Kreuck, Industry; Christopher Rudolph, Shopping and retail design; Daniel Wheeler, Houses and Housing; and Darcy Bonner, Recreation.

Some of the ensembles created by the design architects, and the overall installation coordinated by Tigerman, were quite powerful. For instance, Ron Kreuck's section on industry featured niches created from steel deck-plate that broke up the longitudinal tube (Fig. 7). Dan Wheeler's section on houses and housing, which emphasized the paucity of design thought for low-income residents, became an indictment of architects who tend to work for wealthy clients (Fig. 8). The exhibition opened during the 1993 national convention of the American Institute of Architects (AIA), held in Chicago. It was seen by some 120,000 people and the installation received lively debate in the press, which I consider a sign of success in that the exhibition was thought-provoking.

We are currently planning, with funding from the Driehaus Foundation, a third large exhibition on contemporary Chicago architecture that will be both designed and curated by Chicago architects. Scheduled to be shown in 2004 and again coordinated by Tigerman, the exhibition will have ten theme rooms, each approximately twenty-one feet square, that will represent their designers' projections about the future of Chicago. The ten architects were selected from a group of some twenty competitors invited by a jury that consisted of myself, Associate Curator Martha Thorne, Stanley Tigerman, and Harry Cobb. The design team selected is Jeanne Gang, Douglas Garofalo, Ralph Johnson, Ronald Kreuck, Eva Maddox, Margaret McCurry, Katarina Reudi, Elva Rubio, Joseph Valerio, and Xavier Vendrell. I would venture to guess that the installation will be at least as successful as the other two Chicago exhibitions in terms of creating architectural environments to show visitors that these spaces represent architecture as much as, or even more than, the objects they enshrine.

When the department was created in 1981, its designated exhibition space was Gallery 227, which had been designed in the 1960s by a young Thomas Beeby, then of C.F. Murphy Associates. In this semi-circular gallery of approximately 2,500 square feet, the department actively changed shows three to four times a year, often creating them ourselves. Large shows, such as those designed by Tigerman, were not held in this modest space, but many others were. In 1994, because of our successful exhibition program in Gallery 227, Kisho Kurokawa agreed to generously endow that space. Around this time, encouraged by our success of commissioning architects for major exhibitions, we decided to hire installation designers for even the smallest shows. The first smaller show to benefit from this policy was *The Architecture of Bruce Goff* (1994), curated by Pauline Saliga and installed to the design of Bart Prince, one of Goff's most famous students. Working with a very modest budget, Prince created an undulating roof pattern of nautical rope that simulated the experience of entering one of Goff's organic spaces, and reminded visitors of Goff's creative use of common materials in his work (Fig. 9). Some subsequent exhibition installations that were equally inventive with comparably limited budgets include Nicholas Grimshaw's clever use of steel reinforcing rod panels from road construction to create walls upon which to hang the drawings in the 1995 showing of the Royal Academy's exhibition *Contemporary British Architects*; and Xavier Vendrell's minimalist installation of *Bilbao: Transformation of a City*, curated by Martha Thorne in 2000, which featured wall and floor murals of satellite imagery of Bilbao. We actively raise monies from public and private sources to fund our installations in the Kurokawa Gallery. And, among our many donors, the NEH has consistently supported these public architectural expressions.

The first show supported by the NEH in this space was the 1994 installation of *Karl Friedrich Schinkel, 1781–1841: The Drama of Architecture*. Guest curated by

FIG. 6

STANLEY TIGERMAN

Kiosks in the exhibition store in *Chicago Architecture: 1872–1922*.

FIG. 7

RONALD KREUCK

Installation for the "Industry" section of *Chicago Architecture and Design: 1923–1993*.

RIGHT: FIG. 8

DAN WHEELER

Installation for the "Houses and Housing" section of *Chicago Architecture and Design: 1923–1993*.

Kurt Forster, then director of the Getty Center for Art and Humanities, it featured striking original drawings for buildings and operatic set designs by this important German architect whose work influenced architects well beyond Germany in the nineteenth and twentieth centuries, but whose drawings had never been seen before in the United States. Because of his previous work for

FIG. 9

BART PRINCE

Installation of The Architecture of Bruce Goff, 1904–1982. *Design for the Continuous Present*, shown at the Art Institute of Chicago, June 8 through September 4, 1995.

the department, Stanley Tigerman was selected to design this exhibition. He intended it to feel like walking into one of Schinkel's sepia watercolors. Gary Heitz of Chicago Scenic Studios constructed the installation as he had for a number of our shows. The installation featured Schinkel's original watercolors within a *trompe l'oeil* framework of stenciled pilasters with details taken from

Schinkel's own designs as well as lush drapery that delineated the space into more intimate, opera box-like areas. The colors were kept entirely neutral to match those in Schinkel's own drawings. This classical backdrop was not without inside jokes, typical of many of Stanley Tigerman's structures and spaces. In this case, painted roundels that acted as tie-backs for the drapery and the stenciled wall decorations contained images of a Prussian eagle that metamorphosed into stylized eagles reminiscent of those in 1930s Nazi Germany (Fig. 10).

NEH funding was also critical to the success of two other elaborate installations as well as their related programs and publications. These two exhibitions explored the relationship of architecture, design, and engineering. The first was *Building for Air Travel: Architecture and Design for Commercial Aviation* (1996), which surveyed the airports, aircraft factories, and maintenance facilities that architects, designers, and engineers created, as well as airliner interiors and corporate identities for commercial aviation back to World War I. The exhibition was particularly difficult to curate. Few exhibitable original models and drawings survive from the heroic early period of the 1920s and 1930s, and the only way to represent this work was through vintage photography. Helmut Jahn was chosen to design the show because of his spectacular transportation work, including the United Airlines Terminal at O'Hare, his remodel of the airport at Cologne-Bonn, and the Kempinski Hotel and Munich Airport Center, both at Munich's Franz Josef Strauss International Airport. Jahn created a space that reminded everyone of the importance of the airplane in all of this. The show resembled an abstracted airplane under construction, with striking aluminum ribs that were the visual and sometimes physical framework for the objects on display (Fig. 11). The exhibition attracted record-breaking crowds.

The show spawned a sequel that surveyed similar work for space travel. Organized with the Museum of Flight, *2001: Building for Space Travel* (2001) commemorated the landmark film *2001: A Space Odyssey* (1968) by showing how design professionals worked to create both the reality and fantasy of space travel. Chicago architect Douglas Garofalo created an "alien" environment with stylized moon rocks for pedestals and a wall constructed of disturbingly angular ribs and a metallic skin stretched over strange protrusions (Fig. 12). Indeed, the exhibition

FIG. 10

STANLEY TIGERMAN

Installation of *Karl Friedrich Schinkel, 1781–1841. The Drama of Architecture*, shown at the Art Institute of Chicago, October 29, 1994, through January 2, 1995.

entrance had the sounds of a countdown and a launch and, as the visitor proceeded through the show, that sound receded and the sound of Sputnik morphed into a heartbeat that got louder as one proceeded toward the exit. This exhibit drew an audience of architecture, design, and technology enthusiasts, as well as film and television buffs attracted by the sci-fi artifacts on display,

breaking the attendance totals of *Building for Air Travel*, even rivaling those of our two larger Chicago shows.

The NEH's funding allowed us to present those three projects on a grand scale, but we continue to do other less expensive but equally inventive exhibitions and related projects in the Kurokawa Gallery. The architects on these shows successfully create an appropriate thematic display—for instance, Ralph Johnson's aluminum curtain-wall structure for *Skyscrapers: The New Millennium* (2000); the suggestions of railroad track and train in *Modern Trains and Splendid Stations* (2002) by David Childs and Marilyn Taylor of the New York office of Skidmore, Owings & Merrill (Fig. 13); or Laurence Booth's classicist spatial sequence for country house architect *David Adler* (2002) (Fig. 14). Other shows executed or planned for those spaces include *Aerospace Design* (2003), an exhibition designed by Jeanne Gang and funded principally by NASA, on wind tunnels and wind tunnel models (see p. 234); *Unbuilt Chicago* (2004), to be installed by Daniel Wheeler; and *1945* (2005), an exhibition on architecture and design of the war years designed by Stanley Tigerman to commemorate the sixtieth anniversary of the end of World War II. Beyond that, the future may well hold even greater possibilities as we hope to move

LEFT: FIG. 11

HELMUT JAHN

Installation of *Building for Air Travel: Architecture and Design for Commercial Aviation*, shown at the Art Institute of Chicago, October 19, 1996, through January 5, 1997.

RIGHT: FIG. 12

DOUGLAS GAROFALO

Installation of *2001: Building for Space Travel*, shown at the Art Institute of Chicago, March 24 through October 15, 2001.

our exhibition space into the new wing being designed by Renzo Piano, which is scheduled to open in 2007–8 (see p. 225).

For more than two decades, the Department of Architecture at the Art Institute of Chicago has actively engaged architects from Chicago and beyond, not only through collecting their drawings or in having them lecture, but, even more important, in working with them to create a distinctive exhibition experience for the visitor. These installation architects have helped make the subject of architecture come alive for the general public. They are an integral part of the department's efforts to bring architecture, as much as painting, sculpture, or the decorative arts, to the museum-goer. Those exhibition installations, whether large or small, remind the visitor that architects shape space and suggest that there is an even richer "exhibition" to be found outside the museum's walls. That is, in some ways, the purpose of this book as well. This publication serves to commemorate not just two decades of collecting architectural artwork, but rather a century, and more, of architectural drawings, models, and fragments that exist within the collections of the Art Institute of Chicago—and, more significantly, the treasures that once existed, and still stand, throughout Chicago and its environs. In doing this we are hoping, as in our architect-designed installations, to show the reader that the drawings and models published here are vehicles for creating and understanding the buildings on the city's streets. They are the so-called blueprints intended to help illuminate the bricks and mortar of Chicago.

FIG. 13

SKIDMORE, OWINGS & MERRILL

Installation of *Modern Trains and Splendid Stations*, shown at the Art Institute of Chicago, December 8, 2001, through July 29, 2002.

FIG. 14

LAURENCE BOOTH

Installation of *David Adler, Architect. The Elements of Style*, shown at the Art Institute of Chicago, December 7, 2002, through May 18, 2003.

CITY OF CHI...

PUBLIC COMFORT

FOR PEDESTRIANS TO RECREATION PIER ·
ALSO AN OFFICE ENTRANCE

ENTRANCE TO THE
FREIGHT WAREHOUSES.

STREET CARS ON SUPERSTRUCTURE

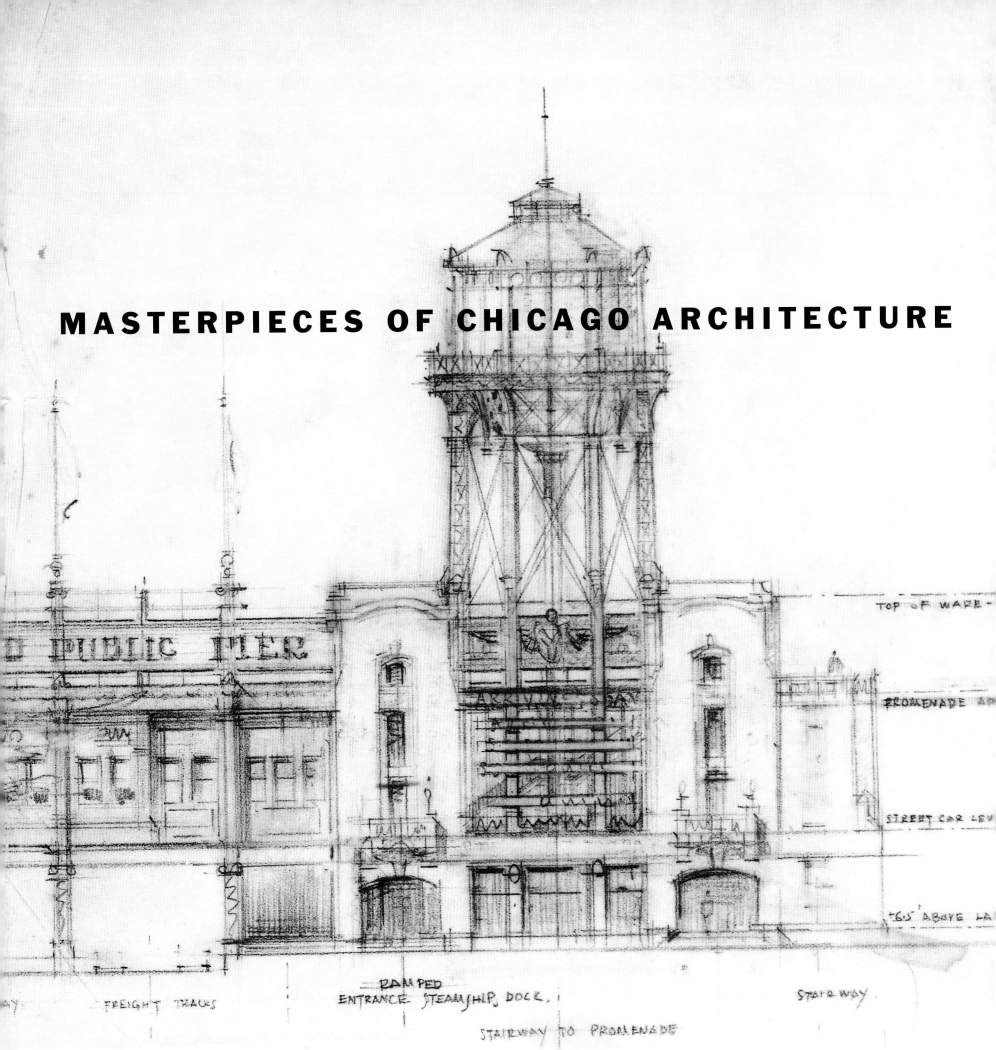

MASTERPIECES OF CHICAGO ARCHITECTURE

STEWART-BENTLEY BUILDING 1872

PETER B. WIGHT

Carter, Drake & Wight

112–114 Dearborn Street, now 30–32 North Dearborn Street

(demolished)

CARTER, DRAKE & WIGHT

Perspective rendering of the
Stewart-Bentley Building, del.
Daniel H. Burnham, 1872.
Ink and watercolor on paper.
Gift of Peter B. Wight.

Lenox Building 1872

PETER B. WIGHT

Carter, Drake & Wight
88–90 Washington Street, now 59 West Washington Street
(demolished)

Peter B. Wight was a New York architect who, after the Chicago Fire of 1871, moved to Chicago to establish his practice. In addition to architecture, Wight worked in other fields as well: he developed a fireproofing system and business in Chicago, and he was a respected architectural writer. When he retired in 1919 he gave the Art Institute his scrapbook of striking original architectural drawings. Daniel H. Burnham and John Wellborn Root had delineated these drawings; indeed, the young architects had met in Wight's office in the early 1870s before starting their own history-making firm of Burnham and Root in 1873. The buildings they drew for Wight's firm are typical of the low-rise, walkup commercial buildings constructed immediately after the 1871 fire—buildings that looked very much like the ones they replaced.

CARTER, DRAKE & WIGHT

Perspective rendering of the Lenox Building, del. John Wellborn Root, 1872. Ink and wash on paper. Gift of Peter B. Wight.

ROOKERY BUILDING 1888

DANIEL H. BURNHAM

Burnham and Root
209 South LaSalle Street

The Rookery Building is one of the great "skyscrapers" of Burnham and Root that still survives. Typical of many of their buildings, this was designed in a variation of Romanesque architecture that became popular throughout the United States after H.H. Richardson built Trinity Church in Boston (1876). The interior, however, is an excellent example of the results of the square-donut plan for offices popularized by Burnham and his followers in subsequent buildings like the Railway Exchange (1903). In this plan, spaces off double-loaded corridors (corridors with offices on both sides) provide the offices with light and air from the street on one side and the central courtyard on the other to the offices. The plan itself enabled a spectacular light court to be built at the Rookery's base—a light court that was probably inspired by similar spaces in Parisian department stores of the era. Frank Lloyd Wright remodeled the interiors in 1905, and a 1990 restoration by McClier Corporation and Takayama & Associates brought the building back to that turn of the century appearance.

BURNHAM AND ROOT

Elevation of the Rookery
Building, 1885. Colored hecto-
graph on paper. Gift of Daniel
Hudson Burnham, Jr.

BURNHAM AND ROOT

Lobby renovated by
Frank Lloyd Wright.

FINE ARTS BUILDING ca. 1890

JOHN WELLBORN ROOT

Burnham and Root
Proposed for the World's Columbian Exposition

When the World's Columbian Exposition of 1893 was first being planned, Burnham and Root were the primary architects, with Burnham in charge of the overall coordination and planning, and Root in charge of design for the prominent buildings. With the sudden death of Root from pneumonia in 1891, major structures such as the

Fine Arts Building were given to other architects, and the overall appearance of the fair became classically oriented, moving away from Root's Romanesque preferences. Burnham appointed Charles Atwood as his head of design, and Atwood created structures at the fair before going on to famous, skeletal Chicago School skyscrapers such as the Reliance Building from 1895. (The Reliance Building was restored in recent years by McClier and Antunovich Associates as the Hotel Burnham.) The drawings shown here project the shift from Root's Romanesque vision to Atwood's, and hence Burnham's, subsequent classical taste, prefiguring what fair observers would dub the "White City."

ABOVE

BURNHAM AND ROOT

Perspective rendering of a proposed Fine Arts Building for the World's Columbian Exposition, del. Paul Lautrup, ca. 1890. Pencil and watercolor on paper. Gift of John Wellborn Root, Jr.

RIGHT

D.H. BURNHAM AND CO.

Palace of Fine Arts, World's Columbian Exposition (later rebuilt as Museum of Science and Industry).

ELEVATION.

SECTION

1/2 PLAN.

3'4"   8'4"   12"   3'4"
15'0"
12"
12"

JAN. 3. 1893.

SCALE 1/2 INCH = 1 FOOT.

·· WORLD'S COLUMBIAN EXPOSITION ··
EXHIBITION PAVILLION
··· FOR MESSRS CLUETT COON AND C.º ···

C.B.ATWOOD. ARCHITECT.

EXHIBITION PAVILION 1893

PETER J. WEBER FOR
CHARLES ATWOOD

D.H. Burnham and Company
Messrs. Cluett Coon and Company
World's Columbian Exposition

RELIANCE BUILDING 1895

CHARLES ATWOOD

D.H. Burnham and Company
1 West Washington

LEFT

D.H. BURNHAM AND COMPANY

Exterior and partial plan of
the Exhibition Pavilion for
Messrs. Cluett Coon and
Company, World's Columbian
Exposition, Jan. 3, 1893.
Blueprint on paper. Gift of
Bertram A. Weber.

RIGHT

D.H. BURNHAM AND COMPANY

Reliance Building.

FISHER BUILDING 1896

PETER J. WEBER

D.H. Burnham and Company
343 South Dearborn Street
Addition 1906

German-born Peter J. Weber worked with the large Berlin firm of Kaiser and von Grossheim before making his way to the Americas, particularly Chicago, in the early 1890s, where he worked for Burnham on buildings for the World's Columbian Exposition of 1893. At D.H. Burnham and Company, he helped to create the Silversmith Building (10 South Wabash Avenue, now Crowne Plaza Hotel) and the famous Fisher Building, both 1896. Weber left Burnham's office in 1900 to start his own practice, and he received the job for an addition to the Fisher Building in 1906–7. His Gothic-styled addition on the north side of the building related contextually to the original building, which was his own design for Burnham.

This landmark has been recently renovated into luxury apartments by the firm of Pappageorge Haymes, known in Chicago for their multifamily residential designs.

D.H. BURNHAM AND COMPANY

Elevation of the addition to
the Fisher Building, 1906.
Ink and colored ink on linen.
Gift of Bertram A. Weber.

D.H. BURNHAM & COMPANY

Entrance and lobby of the
Fisher Building.

TRADING ROOM OF
THE CHICAGO STOCK EXCHANGE 1894

LOUIS H. SULLIVAN

Adler and Sullivan
30 North LaSalle Street (demolished)

Louis H. Sullivan, one of Chicago's great architects, is best known for his approach to ornamental design, which although irregular and anthropomorphic, was quite rational. He believed that there was an underlying geometry that created the bilateral symmetry often found throughout nature. Sullivan's early ornamental studies of the 1870s, when he was a student at the Ecole des Beaux Arts in Paris, were overtly symmetrical but these eventually gave way, in the 1880s and

1890s, to more elaborately expressive designs that culminated in his last flowery ornament on the Krause Music Store and his masterpiece treatise of ornamental design—his *System of Architectural Ornament*, which was, in part, commissioned by the Art Institute of Chicago. The ornamental drawing for the McVickers Theatre shown on page 48 was found in a book on the Franco-Prussian War that was once in Sullivan's library.

Adler and Sullivan

Trading Room of the Chicago Stock Exchange, 1893–94 (demolished 1972); reconstructed in The Art Institute of Chicago, 1976–77, supervised by Vinci-Kenny Architects.
The reconstruction and reinstallation of the Trading Room were made possible through a grant from the Walter E. Heller Foundation and its president, Mrs. Edwin J. DeCosta, with additional gifts from the City of Chicago, Mrs. Eugene A. Davidson, The Graham Foundation for Advanced Studies in the Fine Arts, and Three Oaks Wrecking.

SCHLESINGER AND MAYER STORE (NOW CARSON PIRIE SCOTT) 1899

LOUIS H. SULLIVAN

1 South State Street

RIGHT

LOUIS H. SULLIVAN

Section of a screen from the third-floor writing room of the Schlesinger and Mayer Store, 1899. Five layers of fret-sawn mahogany. Gift of George Fred Keck.

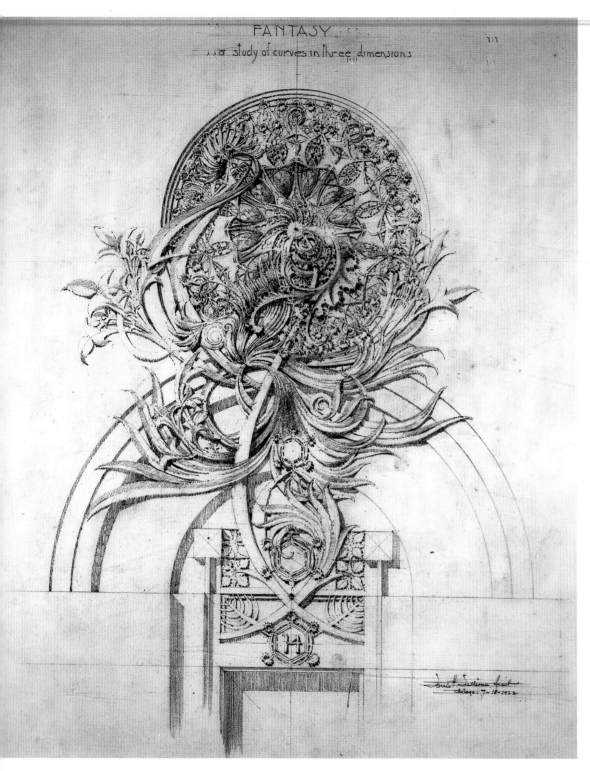

FANTASY

...a study of curves in three dimensions

MCVICKERS THEATRE c. 1891

LOUIS H. SULLIVAN

78–84 Madison Street (demolished)

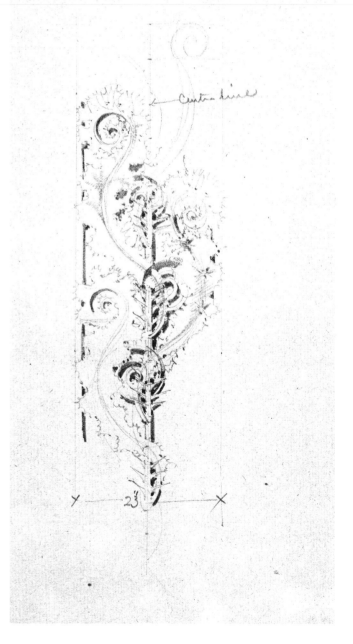

LOUIS H. SULLIVAN

Original artwork for Plate 14, "The Inorganic: Development of a blank block through a series of mechanical manipulations which illustrate Man's initial control over materials and their Destiny," from *A System of Architectural Ornament, According with a Philosophy of Man's Powers, 1922*. Pencil on Strathmore. Partly commissioned by the Art Institute of Chicago.

LOUIS H. SULLIVAN

Ornamental sketch, McVickers Theatre, ca. 1883–91. Graphite on paper. Restricted gift of the Director's Fund Committee on Acquisitions.

Krause Music Store 1922

Louis H. Sullivan

4611 North Lincoln Avenue

Louis H. Sullivan

Krause Music Store.

FULLER ("FLATIRON") BUILDING 1902

FREDERICK P. DINKELBERG

Daniel H. Burnham and Company
23rd Street and Broadway, New York

Chicago's Daniel H. Burnham and Company was one of America's most influential and successful architectural firms, with buildings designed and built from coast to coast, as well as abroad in Canada, the Philippines, and England. One of their most famous outside of Chicago is the Flatiron Building in New York, designed, in part, by Frederick P. Dinkelberg in Burnham's office—a designer who also worked on Burnham buildings in Chicago like the Railway Exchange (1903) and Conway Building (1912). Rendered here in a dramatic view by Jules Guérin, the building is more typical of Chicago skyscrapers than of those in New York. Its 22 stories, some 300 feet high, were built out to the lot line so the building lacks the pronounced slender tower that characterizes many New York buildings of the period. In a letter to Burnham (April 30, 1902), prominent New York architect Charles McKim wrote that only the "Tower of Babel" was higher than Burnham's building. The Flatiron was captured in the artistic expressions of photographers such as Alfred Steiglitz and Edward Steichen, and it is responsible for the popular phrase "twenty-three skidoo," which is what police officers said to chase away the girlwatchers around the building, who had learned that the high-rise's downdraft caused women's skirts to blow around.

DANIEL H. BURNHAM AND COMPANY

Perspective rendering of the Flatiron Building, del. Jules Guérin, 1902. Charcoal and ink wash on underpainted linen. Restricted gift of the Thomas J. and Mary E. Eyerman Foundation.

THE PLAN OF CHICAGO 1909

DANIEL H. BURNHAM AND EDWARD H. BENNETT

Daniel H. Burnham, often with the assistance of Edward H. Bennett, created a number of master plans for cities at the turn of the century, including San Francisco and Cleveland (both 1905), but the duo's masterpiece was *The Plan of Chicago*, commissioned by the Commercial Club. In it they proposed that Chicago could be as beautiful as any European city and, thus, as commercially successful. Burnham's draftsmen did the spectacular presentation drawings for this plan to make Chicago a Paris on the prairie, with French architect Fernand Janin preparing ink and wash presentations for a new domed City Hall at the Civic Center, and Jules Guérin, a

ABOVE

DANIEL H. BURNHAM AND EDWARD H. BENNETT

The Plan of Chicago drawings on exhibition in Düsseldorf, August 1910, from Charles Moore, *Daniel H. Burnham* (1921).

DANIEL H. BURNHAM AND EDWARD H. BENNETT

The Plan of Chicago, 1909: Chicago. Presentation drawing of the Proposed Civic Center, del. Jules Guérin. Ink, colored inks, graphite, and watercolor on toned paper.

Gift of Edward H. Bennett, Jr.

renderer from New York, providing some of the more spectacular impressionist watercolor and tempera visions of this city. The drawings were exhibited at the Art Institute of Chicago in 1909, and the success of that presentation led to their being shown as far away as London and Düsseldorf, epitomizing Burnham's famous quote, "Make no little plans; they have no magic to stir men's blood. . . ."

After Burnham's death in 1912, Bennett helped to popularize what was called the "City Beautiful" movement throughout North America with comparable plans for cities such as Portland, Oregon (1913), Ottawa and Hull in Canada (1914), Detroit (1915), Minneapolis (1917), Phoenix (1921), and Pasadena (1923), among others.

DANIEL H. BURNHAM AND EDWARD H. BENNETT

Plate 87, "View looking west over the city, showing the proposed Civic Center, the Grand Axis, and the Harbor," *The Plan of Chicago*, 1909, del. Jules Guérin. Watercolor and graphite on paper. Gift of Patrick Shaw.

ROCK CREST/ROCK GLEN ca. 1912

WALTER BURLEY GRIFFIN AND MARION MAHONY GRIFFIN

Mason City, Iowa

Walter Burley Griffin and his wife, Marion Mahony Griffin, were architects who both worked for Frank Lloyd Wright and designed Prairie Style homes for their own clients. An important Prairie subdivision they created in Mason City, Iowa, is shown in this spectacular rendering that is typical of Marion's drawings; it is essentially a painting on printed fabric that suggests an almost Japanese style. When the Griffins won the 1912 compe-

tition to design Canberra, Australia's capitol, they moved to Melbourne and established a successful practice there. They relocated again to India in 1936 to work on Lucknow University and the United Provinces Exhibition of Industry and Agriculture in Lucknow. They were thus responsible for exporting their version of America's Prairie Style—a style with Asian influences—back to the Far East.

ABOVE

WALTER BURLEY GRIFFIN AND MARION MAHONY GRIFFIN

Bird's-eye view of Rock Crest/Rock Glen, Mason City, Iowa, ca. 1912. Lithograph and gouache on green satin.
Gift of Marion Mahony Griffin.

RIGHT

ROY LIPPINCOTT AND MARION MAHONY GRIFFIN

Perspective of Soldiers Club, Toowomba, Queensland, Australia, 1919. Ink on linen.
Gift of Marion Mahony Griffin through Eric Nichols.

AVERY COONLEY PLAYHOUSE 1912

FRANK LLOYD WRIGHT

350 Fairbanks Road, Riverside, Illinois

Frank Lloyd Wright is considered by many to be America's greatest architect. He was the leading proponent of the Prairie Style of residential design—homes with open, horizontally rambling spaces that related to the gently rolling hills of Wisconsin's landscape, the landscape of Wright's home. When Wright first started out on his own, after working for Adler and Sullivan in the late 1880s, he designed a number of houses in Oak Park, Illinois, where he lived at the time, as well as in nearby Chicago suburbs such as River Forest and Riverside. One of the most important of these was the Avery Coonley House (1908) in Riverside. He later created a small structure to house a progressive school established by Mrs. Coonley for her daughter, Elizabeth. This Coonley Playhouse recalls Wright's early Prairie homes, though it has very different windows. The windows' colored circles, American flags, and small colored and clear squares and rectangles were all intended to evoke the balloons, flags, and confetti of a parade. Although these striking windows were removed in the 1960s and have made their way into museums around the country, the Coonley Playhouse itself was restored by architect John Vinci in the late 1980s, complete with replica windows created by Oakbrook Esser Studios.

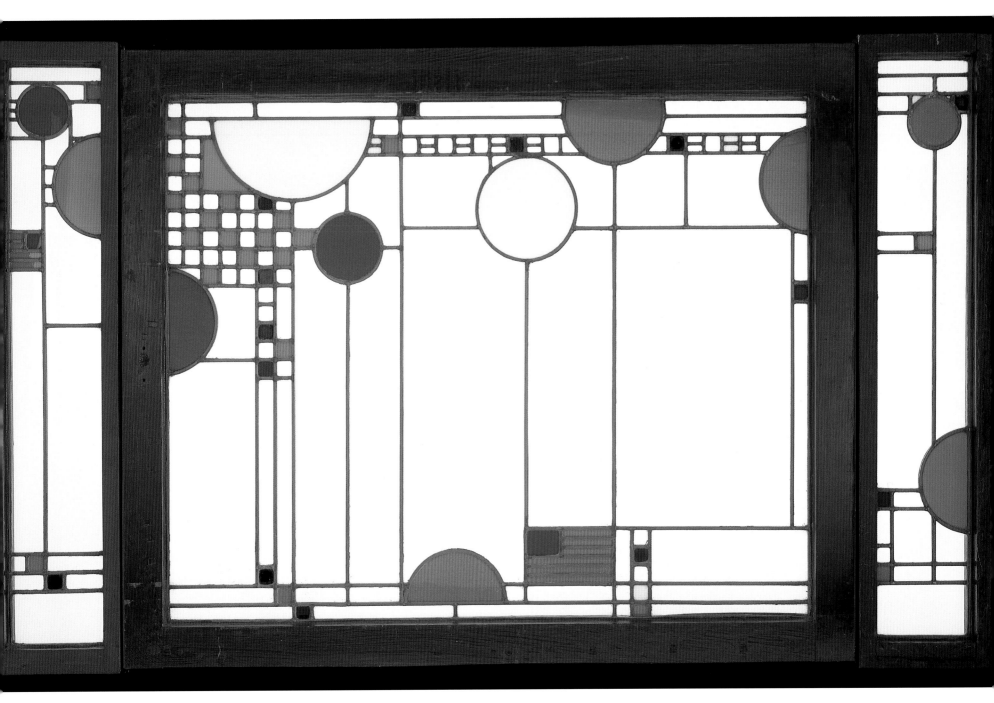

FRANK LLOYD WRIGHT

Triptych window from a
niche in the Avery Coonley
Playhouse, 1912. Clear and
leaded glass. Restricted gift of
the Walter E. Heller Foundation and
Dr. and Mrs. Edwin J. De Costa.

HEAD HOUSE, CHICAGO MUNICIPAL PIER (NOW NAVY PIER) 1916

CHARLES SUMNER FROST

Benjamin Thompson Associates, associate architects
Renovation 1995
VOA Associates, Inc.

When Navy Pier first opened in 1916 as the Municipal Pier, it served as a multiuse entertainment facility as well as a public pier, but during the First and Second World Wars it functioned, respectively, as barracks for several regiments of troops and as a training base for Navy mechanics, technicians, and pilots. From 1946 to 1965 the University of Illinois used the facility, named Navy Pier in 1927, as an urban campus though it still functioned as a pier for local steamers and served, increasingly in the 1970s and 1980s, as a convention, trade fair, and entertainment center.

Today, after an extensive renovation, Navy Pier has become one of Chicago's great tourist attractions, with more than 8 million visitors a year. This mega-entertainment center, complete with Shakespearean theater, children's museum, IMAX theater, restaurants, and stores, was developed in 1992 through a national design competition that was won by VOA, a Chicago firm, with BTA of Cambridge, Massachusetts. They used the Navy Pier as the basis for their complex, which was designed to reshape a disused waterfront facility much as was done, in the 1970s and 1980s, at sites throughout the United States such as South Street Seaport in New York, Fanueil Hall in Boston, and Baltimore's Inner Harbor.

3400 North Sheridan Road 1917

PETER J. WEBER
White and Weber

German-born and -trained Peter J. Weber came to Chicago to work for Burnham's firm at the time of the World's Columbian Exposition of 1893. After gaining experience designing a number of Burnham's commercial and institutional buildings, Weber went off on his own in 1900 to create like-scaled constructions such as the Seattle Public Library (1903–4, demolished) and the Dry Goods Reporter Building in Chicago (1908–9, demolished). One of his more striking highrises is the classically styled apartment building at 3400 North Sheridan Road, designed before America's entry into World War I but constructed after the war in 1921. In its scale and elaborate classical detailing it was similar to other apartment buildings along Chicago's lakefront in the boom era of the 1920s.

RIGHT

WHITE AND WEBER

Perspective rendering for 3400 North Sheridan Road, initialed L.R., ca. 1915–17. Pencil and gouache on illustration board. Gift of Bertram Weber.

RICHARD YOSHIJIRO MINE

Competitive entry (elevation) to the Chicago Tribune Competition, 1922. Ink and wash on paper. Gift of Richard Yoshijiro Mine.

CHICAGO TRIBUNE TOWER COMPETITION
1922

In 1922 the *Chicago Tribune* announced an international competition to design its headquarters, which it envisioned as the world's most beautiful building. Some might argue that by 1920s standards the building chosen, a striking tower inspired by the medieval *Tour de buerre* of Rouen, France (see pp. 66–67), was not necessarily the world's most beautiful Gothic high-rise, a title more correctly given to the Woolworth Building in New York (1914). Yet the competition itself was probably much more important than the building it generated. A massive book with the competitive entries was circulated around the globe. Of the more than 250 entries received, more than 100 came from architects outside the United States, including such up and coming international stars as Walter Gropius, Bruno Taut, and Max Taut, all from Germany, Eliel Saarinen of Finland, and Adolf Loos, from France. Of all of them, Saarinen's is perhaps the most important because his setback modernist skyscraper foreshadowed other such creations throughout the U.S. in the later 1920s. The jury gave a number of honorable mentions, one of which went to Japanese-American Richard Yoshijiro Mine, who used the Woolworth Building as inspiration for his design. The Art Institute's collection has his entry as well as several others but, mysteriously, most of the final drawings never resurfaced after the *Chicago Tribune* circulated an exhibition of those great renderings in the 1920s.

LEFT

R. Harold Zook

Competitive entry (perspective view) to the Chicago Tribune Tower Competition, 1922. Ink and wash on paper. Gift of Robert H. Reinhold through prior gift of the Three Oaks Wrecking Company.

RIGHT

Ralph Walker

Competitive entry (study elevation) for the Chicago Tribune Competition, 1922. Pencil on tracing paper. Gift of Haines Lundberg and Waehler in honor of their centennial.

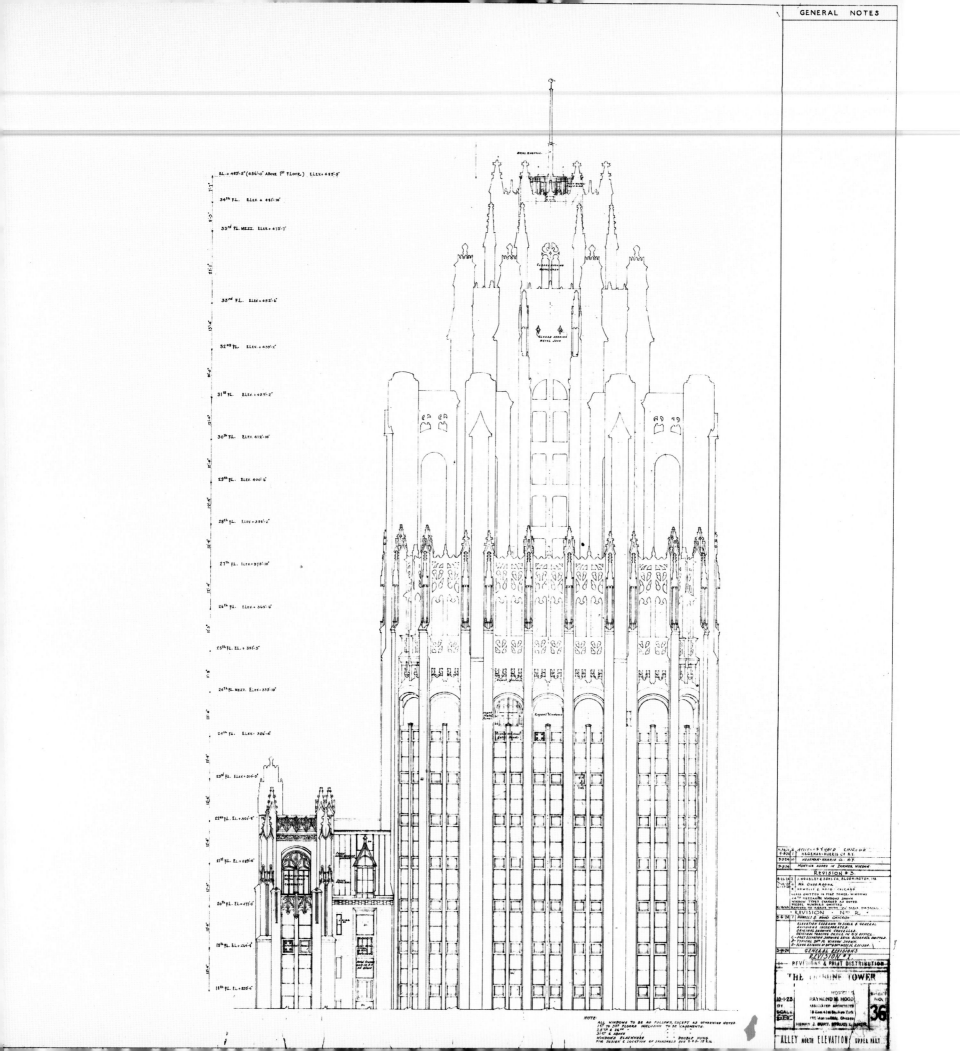

CHICAGO TRIBUNE TOWER 1925

HOWELLS AND HOOD

435 N. Michigan Avenue

LEFT

HOWELLS AND HOOD

North elevation of the 18th to 34th floors of the Chicago Tribune Tower, October 1, 1923 (sheet 36). Blueprinted paper. Gift of Howells and Hood.

LONDON GUARANTEE AND ACCIDENT BUILDING 1923

ALFRED S. ALSCHULER

360 North Michigan Avenue

The 1909 *Plan of Chicago* included provisions for widening Pine Street into a Parisian-style boulevard, to be named Michigan Avenue, and for building a new bridge to span the Chicago River at that site. When the bridge, designed by Edward H. Bennett, was built in 1918–20, the land at its base became one of the most important intersections in Chicago, catalyzed by the 1921–24 construction of the Wrigley Building by architects Graham, Anderson, Probst & White. With the competition for the nearby Chicago Tribune tower announced and under way (see p. 64), it was only natural that another parcel near the bridge would quickly be developed, this time for the London Guarantee and Accident Company, on what was originally part of the historic Fort Dearborn (ca. 1803), Chicago's first settlement.

Alfred S. Alschuler designed the sturdy limestone Greco-Roman building in accordance with Chicago's zoning law, which stated that any part of a building higher than 260 feet must be unoccupied, hence the classical cupola atop. (The law was later changed for construction of the 1925 Chicago Tribune Tower.) The London Guarantee Building went through some modernizations after World War II, and a recent restoration of the building by Lohan Associates included the incorporation of the original Fort Dearborn relief sculpture above its entrance.

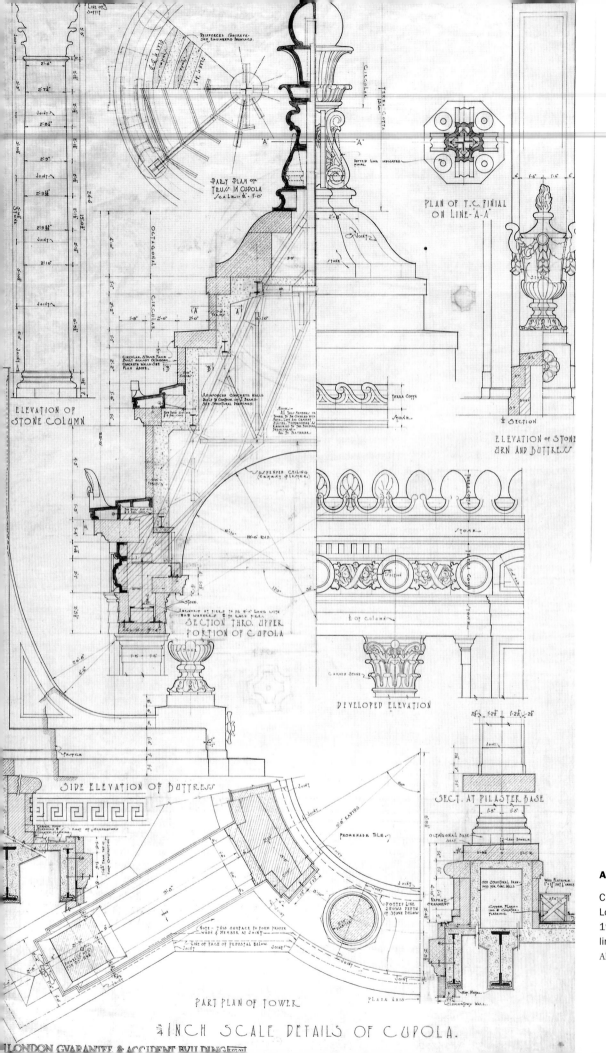

ALFRED S. ALSCHULER

Cupola elevation of the
London Guarantee Building,
1922 (sheet 22). Ink on
linen. Gift of Friedman,
Alschuler, Sincere.

PALMER HOUSE 1925–27

HOLABIRD AND ROCHE

Monroe and State Streets, and Wabash Avenue

The Palmer House is Chicago's most famous historic hotel. Famed Chicago businessman Potter Palmer opened the first hotel on this site in 1870. Destroyed in the Great Fire of 1871, the Empire Style building was reconstructed to an even grander scheme in 1872, with 700 rooms and extensive services, setting the standard for luxury hotels in the city. Potter Palmer and his architect John Van Osdel had toured Europe to see the grand hotels of Paris and London before designing the second Palmer House.

The current Palmer House, by Holabird and Roche, attempted to top its predecessor by incorporating a virtual history of French architecture in its rooms, the most famous of which is the Napoleonic Empire Room. The Empire style decorating scheme shown in the drawing was altered in its details during construction, though the room retained the overall concept portrayed in the drawing. Although the hotel, now part of the Hilton chain, was renovated in the 1960s and 1980s, the Empire Room and opulent Renaissance style lobby have been restored to their grandeur.

HOLABIRD AND ROCHE

Main lobby.

HOLABIRD AND ROCHE

Perspective renderings of the lobby (above) and Empire Style dining room (right) with proposed decoration, Palmer House, del. Mack, Jenny & Tyler Decorators, 1925. Watercolor on illustration board. Restricted gift of the Benefactors of Architecture.

BOULEVARD APARTMENTS ca. 1925

HENRY DUBIN

Dubin and Eisenberg

Although not representative of any singular landmark, this perspective study is important because it represents a ubiquitous Chicago building type: the low-rise, walkup, courtyard apartment building seen throughout the city's neighborhoods dating to David Postle's famous Pattington Apartments (1902) on 660 Irving Park Road. The architect of the Boulevard Apartments, Henry Dubin, achieved local prominence as the designer of a number of residential structures including the Battledeck House in Highland Park (1929–30), a home made from welded steel like the deck of a battleship. The drawing is significant as an example of the distinctive delineation of Charles Morgan. As seen in this work, Morgan typically used crushed paper that he then flattened and affixed to a board, creating a textured surface for his rendering.

LEFT

DUBIN AND EISENBERG

Perspective rendering of the Boulevard Apartments (unbuilt), del. Charles Morgan, ca. 1925. Pencil, chalk, and watercolor, mounted on board. Gift of Dubin, Dubin and Moutoussamy.

BELOW

DAVID POSTLE

Pattington Apartments.

BUCKINGHAM FOUNTAIN 1927

BENNETT, PARSONS, THOMAS & FROST

Congress Drive at Columbus Drive

Buckingham Fountain is, in many ways, one of the great symbols of Chicago. Designed by Edward H. Bennett, co-creator of the famous *Plan of Chicago* (1909, see p. 52), and his partners in Bennett, Parsons, Thomas & Frost, with seahorse sculptures by Marcel Loyau, the fountain was inspired by the Latona Basin in the gardens at Versailles. Kate Buckingham donated Chicago's fountain as a memorial to her brother. Built of pink Georgia marble, it underwent a major restoration in 1994. The fountain sits at the center of Grant Park at the site Bunham and Bennett, proposed for the Field Museum in their *Plan*. However, a successful lawsuit by mail-order merchant A. Montgomery Ward, which cited early city ordinances that the park was to be free of permanent buildings, forced the construction of the Field Museum—named for rival merchant Marshall Field—to the south end of Grant Park.

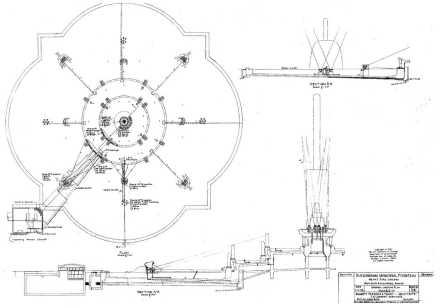

ABOVE

**BENNETT, PARSONS,
THOMAS & FROST**

Perspective study of
Buckingham Fountain, signed
by Cyrus W. Thomas, 1923.
Pencil on paper, highlighted
with gouache/China white.
Through prior gift of Three Oaks
Wrecking Company.

LEFT

Plan, section, elevation,
and details of Buckingham
Fountain, May 6, 1925.
Ink on linen. Gift of Edward H.
Bennett, Jr.

1500 LAKE SHORE DRIVE 1928

JAMES EDWIN QUINN

McNally and Quinn

In the 1910s and 1920s Chicago witnessed the construction of many luxury apartment buildings, particularly on the desirable waterfront off Lake Shore Drive and its northern extension, Sheridan Road. A prominent example of this type of high-rise is 1500 Lake Shore Drive by McNally and Quinn. This small firm established itself among those doing such buildings. Its other work included: 399 Fullerton Parkway, and 1366 North Dearborn Street (both 1926); 3240 Sheridan Road (1927); 73 East Elm Street and 415 Fullerton Parkway (both 1928); and 1100 North Dearborn Street and 2000 Lincoln Park West (both 1929). The Great Depression of the 1930s destroyed the firm; partner James Edwin Quinn practiced after World War II as an architect for the Cook County Highway system (see p. 106).

McNally and Quinn
Perspective rendering of
1500 Lake Shore Drive, del.
B.C. Greengard, ca. 1925.
Printed paper. Gift of James
Edwin Quinn.

ABOVE

McNally and Quinn
Perspective rendering of
the penthouse for George
Woodruff atop 1500 Lake
Shore Drive, Chicago, 1928
(executed somewhat differ-
ently), del. George A.
Hossack. Pencil on paper.
Gift of James Edwin Quinn.

CARBIDE AND CARBON BUILDING 1929

DANIEL BURNHAM JR. AND HUBERT BURNHAM

D.H. Burnham and Co. (The Burnham Brothers)
230 North Michigan Avenue

Burnham's sons, Daniel Jr. and Hubert, became architects who worked in the family firm. After the father's death in 1912, that firm gradually split into two successor organizations. One, headed by Ernest Graham, became Graham, Burnham and Company (later Graham, Anderson, Probst & White). The other, directed by his sons, continued the name D.H. Burnham and Company from 1917 to 1929, when they changed it to Burnham Brothers. The sons designed classically detailed high rises such as the Bankers Building (1926) and the Engineering Building (1928). In the Carbide and Carbon Building, however, they made a significant departure from that tradition by creating a dynamic black, green, and gold-toned Art Deco skyscraper of brick and terracotta with an overall appearance that many say derives from the like-styled American Radiator Building (1924) in New York by Raymond Hood. Originally the regional headquarters of Union Carbide, the maker of Eveready batteries, the Burnhams' building was recently remodeled by architect Lucien LaGrange and reopened as a Hard Rock Hotel in 2004.

**D.H. BURNHAM AND CO.
(THE BURNHAM BROTHERS)**

Perspective study of the
Carbide and Carbon Building,
1927–28. Pencil on tracing
paper. Restricted gift of the
Architecture Society and Friends of
the Library in honor of the Seventy-
Fifth Anniversary of the Burnham
Library of Architecture.

North West Tower 1929

Perkins, Chatten & Hammond

1608 North Milwaukee Avenue

In 1925 the firm Perkins, Chatten & Hammond was established by Dwight H. Perkins, Melvin C. Chatten, and C. Herrick Hammond as the successor to the thirty-year-old firm of Perkins, Fellows & Hamilton. The new firm carried on the tradition of sensible design and quality construction. The North West Tower, located in the Wicker Park neighborhood, was touted as the "finest most up-to-date office building on the northwest side" in a 1929 issue of *Greater Chicago Magazine* (vol. 4, no. 2, page 9).

The building was developed by a corporation owned by the Noel State Bank, a leading developer of the Wicker Park district, since its establishment there in 1905. In 1924 businessmen of the area formed the Milwaukee, North, and Robey Improvement Association (which became the local Chamber of Commerce) to put the area "on the map." Undoubtedly, the landmark North West Tower was an important and visible part of their improvement campaign.

The tower, which emphasizes its verticality the composition of facades and elongated windows, is located on a triangular corner site. The two main 12-story facades, constructed of granite and limestone, line North and Milwaukee Avenues. At the corner, the tower is really a stone cupola crowned by a bronze lantern rising even higher to 180 feet. The same issue of *Greater Chicago Magazine* noted, "The observatory on the elevator penthouse is an innovation for this district and will be open to the public. The height makes it possible to see the lake from the observatory. . . . The beacon will serve to advertise the entire district."

Perkins, Chatten & Hammond

Perspective view of North West Tower, ca. 1928. Graphite on tracing paper.

Through prior gift of Three Oaks Wrecking Company.

FIELD BUILDING
(NOW LaSALLE NATIONAL BANK) 1931

ALFRED SHAW

Graham, Anderson, Probst & White
135 South LaSalle Street

Graham, Anderson, Probst & White created a number of the city's most important buildings in the 1920s including the Wrigley Building (1921), the Merchandise Mart (1923–31), the Shedd Aquarium (1923–29), and the Civic Opera House (1929). They also built the Field Building (1934), funded by the estate of retailer Marshall Field, during the Great Depression. Part of the Field Building site occupied the location of William LeBaron Jenney's Home Insurance Building of 1884—often said to have been the first skyscraper. The Field's architects, with their designer Alfred Shaw, created an Art Moderne masterpiece of conservative modernism in their 40-story tower of Indiana limestone. Its dramatic five-story entrance with subdued classical detailing was rendered for the building's publicity booklet by Henry Harringer, a Hamburg architect who left Germany and its runaway inflation for Chicago in the mid-1920s to continue his career in retail and advertising design.

GRAHAM, ANDERSON, PROBST & WHITE

Perspective study of the entrance to the Field Building, del. Henry Harringer, ca. 1930–31. Charcoal and pencil on tracing. Gift of Olaf Harringer.

THE ATTIC CLUB 1935

DAVID ADLER

David Adler, Architect
Field Building
135 South LaSalle Street

David Adler designed the interiors of a private club located on the 43rd and 44th floors in the Field Building in downtown Chicago. When built in 1934 by Graham, Anderson, Probst & White, the Field Building was conceived as the Loop's largest office building. With four lower structures at the corners and a central tower rising above, the overall décor of the building was inspired by Art Deco.

The Attic Club, in the invitations extended to potential members, billed itself as "a club which is to be union of the artists, art lovers, and literary men of Chicago, somewhat like the Players Club of New York City. . . . We plan to have a home of our own near the Fine Arts Building (possibly on the top of some building) with our own kitchen and grill room and with unique and tasteful furnishings."

David Adler, noted Chicago architect of some of the North Shore's most stately homes, was commissioned

DAVID ADLER, ARCHITECT

East elevation of the interior of the Attic Club in the Field Building, 1933. Graphite on tracing paper. Gift of Bowen Blair, executor of the estate of William McCormick Blair.

to design the club. Although Adler often relied on traditional historical models for the design of houses, the Attic Club is decidedly modern. The sleek, curved staircase that connects the upper-level private dining rooms with the main dependencies on the 43rd floor closely resembles earlier staircases by French modernist Robert Mallet-Stevens. The decoration of the club has its strength in the varied materials and surface treatments rather than in elaborate moldings and other traditional details. The floor of the main dining room is inlaid with a pattern of elongated six-pointed stars. The oyster bar has walls of marble and a geometrically patterned floor. The predominant decorations for the main dining room are the dark wainscoting and the upper-level balcony enclosed by simple wrought-iron railings. The only classical details that Adler added are the vases resting on sleek black columns.

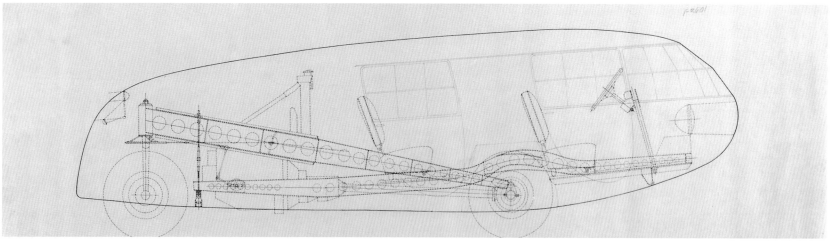

DYMAXION CAR ca. 1933

R. BUCKMINSTER FULLER

Century of Progress Exposition

The dramatic advances in transportation from 1833 to 1933 were featured at the Century of Progress Exposition (1933–34) in the regular performances of the pageant "Wings of a Century," as well as in the concurrent development of streamlined trains and cars such as the Burlington Zephyr and Dymaxion Car. In fact, Boeing and United Airlines exhibited their latest airliner within the angular, modernist Travel and Transport Building. Visitors could see the new streamlined Boeing 247 up

close, which could whisk ten passengers to their destinations in air-conditioned comfort at a speed over 180 miles per hour. The culmination of transportation pageantry at the fair came on July 15, 1933. Over a million fairgoers saw Italian general Italo Balbo land his squadron of seaplanes on Lake Michigan following a transatlantic flight. They came to dedicate an antique Roman column that Mussolini gave to the people of Chicago—a column that still stands today near Soldier Field.

EDWARD H. BENNETT, JOHN HOLABIRD, AND HUBERT BURNHAM

Century of Progress Exposition

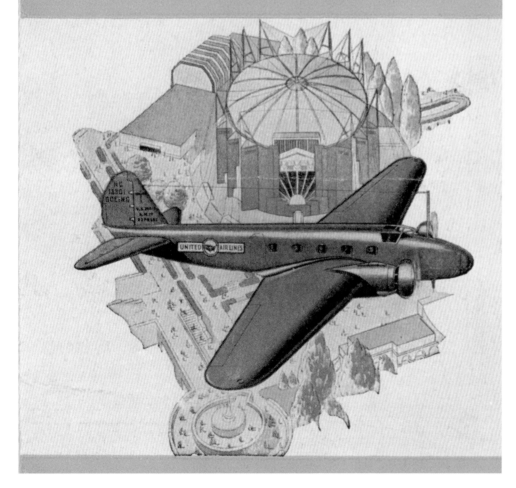

UNITED AIR LINES

New Type All-Metal Wasp-Powered "Three-Mile-A-Minute" Boeing Transport displayed in the Dome of the TRAVEL AND TRANSPORT BUILDING, Chicago, 1933

Travel and Transport Building shown on a United Airlines schedule, 1933.

EDWARD H. BENNETT

Night rendering of the
Travel and Transport
Building, Century of Progress
Exposition, del. attrib. Robert
Spaulding, ca. 1930–32.
Graphite and charcoal on
illustration board. Through
prior gift of Three Oaks Wrecking
Company.

VOORHEES, GMELIN & WALKER

Perspective rendering of the
final design of the Proposed
Tower of Water and Light,
Century of Progress
Exposition, del. John Wenrich,
1930. Pencil and watercolor
on illustration board. Gift of
Haines, Lundberg and Waehler in
honor of their Centennial.

PROPOSED TOWER OF WATER AND LIGHT

1930

RALPH WALKER

Voorhees, Gmelin & Walker
Century of Progress Exposition

The Century of Progress Exposition (1933–34) was unique in that it was a major world's fair that was financed almost completely with private monies, an especially remarkable accomplishment since it was held during the Great Depression. New York architect Ralph Walker along with Chicagoans Hubert Burnham, Edward H. Bennett, and John Holabird, and Philadelphian Paul Cret were among those who created the overall plan of the exposition in the late 1920s and designed some of the actual buildings in the fair. Joseph Urban was their color consultant. Of the structures planned for the fair but

Sky-Ride, designed by Louis Skidmore and Nathaniel Owings.

unexecuted, perhaps the most spectacular was the Tower of Water and Light. Walker intended it to be the center-piece of the fair, a skyscraper-like sculpture of concrete and glass with water cascading down. Wenrich's dramatic rendering includes an airship and aircraft—high-tech symbols of the era. Because the tower offered few opportunities to generate income, the fair commission opted instead to build the now-famous Sky-Ride, the first work of young architects Louis Skidmore and Nathaniel Owings, partners who shortly thereafter started the successful firm of Skidmore Owings & Merrill.

MRS. KERSEY COATS REED HOUSE 1932

DAVID ADLER

David Adler, Architect
Lake Road, Lake Forest, Illinois

Milwaukee-born David Adler (1882–1949) was the residential architect of choice for Chicago's wealthy families for three decades beginning in about 1915. Trained at Princeton and the Ecole des Beaux Arts in Paris, he drew on a variety of historical sources to create his perfectly proportioned homes. More than a dozen were built on Chicago's North Shore, while others can be found across the country, from Massachusetts to Hawaii.

The house for Mrs. Kersey Coats Reed is one of Adler's finest. Inspired by Cliveden just outside Philadelphia, this middle-Georgian style home is constructed of gray, mica-flecked stone, with contrasting white painted moldings and shutters, and a slate roof. The 224-foot-long main facade of the house is symmetrically composed with a main central block. Smaller volumes with gambrel roofs act as hyphens that connect with paired side wings. Adler cleverly focuses attention on the main part of the house by visually separating it from the service wing with the stone wall around the perimeter.

The interior exemplifies Adler's eclecticism through his use of modern and traditional elements. The decoration, undertaken with his sister and collaborator Frances Elkins, incorporates sleek modern furnishings of the 1920s and geometric floor patterns in some rooms, along with classically inspired moldings and antique wallpapers in others.

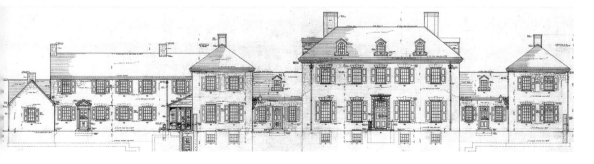

DAVID ADLER, ARCHITECT

Elevation of Kersey Coates Reed House, 1931. Ink on linen; graphite, colored pencil, and colored ink added.
Gift of Bowen Blair, executor of the estate of William McCormick Blair.

NORTHWESTERN MEMORIAL HOSPITAL

MONTGOMERY WARD MEMORIAL BUILDING 1926

JAMES GAMBLE ROGERS

Childs & Smith, associate architects
303–311 East Chicago Avenue

Renowned collegiate Gothic architect James Gamble Rogers, known for the Harkness Memorial Quadrangle at Yale (1921), designed the 18-story Gothic revival Montgomery Ward Memorial Building, as the centerpiece of Northwestern University's hospital complex. Labeled as the first skyscraper university building to be completed in the United States, it was one of the first of several high-rise hospital structures on this urban campus, which included work over the next decades by architects such as Thielbar and Fugard; Schmidt, Garden & Erickson; Bertrand Goldberg Associates; Holabird and Root; and Perkins and Will. Some of the older buildings in this complex—particularly the pictured Wesley Memorial Hospital—were demolished in 2003 to make way for more advanced facilities in this ever-growing medical center.

LEFT

JAMES GAMBLE ROGERS

Perspective view of
Montgomery Ward Memorial
Building, looking at Chicago
Avenue entrance, del. James
G. Rogers, n.d. Watercolor
and ink over graphite with
Chinese white added, on
paper mounted on cardboard.
Through prior gift of Three Oaks
Wrecking Company.

RIGHT

Lobby of Montgomery Ward
Memorial Building.

WESLEY MEMORIAL HOSPITAL 1941

THIELBAR AND FUGARD

Superior Street and Fairbanks Court (demolished)

THIELBAR AND FUGARD

Perspective study of Wesley Memorial Hospital (Wesley Pavilion of Northwestern Memorial Hospital), del. F. Holcomb, ca. 1935. Pencil and watercolor on paper, mounted on illustration board. Gift of Fugard, Orth & Associates.

HERBERT A. JACOBS HOUSE 1944

FRANK LLOYD WRIGHT

Middleton, Wisconsin

Although Frank Lloyd Wright is best known for his Prairie Style residences, he had several creative periods in his long design life. In the 1930s and 1940s he developed Usonian Homes, affordable residences that eventually led to the ubiquitous ranch homes of the post–World War II American suburb. One of the first Usonian Homes was built for Herbert and Katherine Jacobs in Madison, Wisconsin (1937). Shortly after he designed and built the first Jacobs house, Wright began working on another home for the family that was more curvilinear in plan, similar to the Guggenheim Museum in New York that he was designing at the same time. The second Jacobs home was also directly related to Wright's long-term interest in exploring the relationship between interior and exterior spaces. By building the stone and glass house within a berm of the hillside he made the house appear integral to the landscape. The convex, submerged side of the house, which contains the bedrooms, faces north and conserves energy, keeping the house warm in the winter and cool in the summer. Likewise, the concave glass facade faces south to the sun, acting as a passive solar device for the public spaces of living and dining rooms.

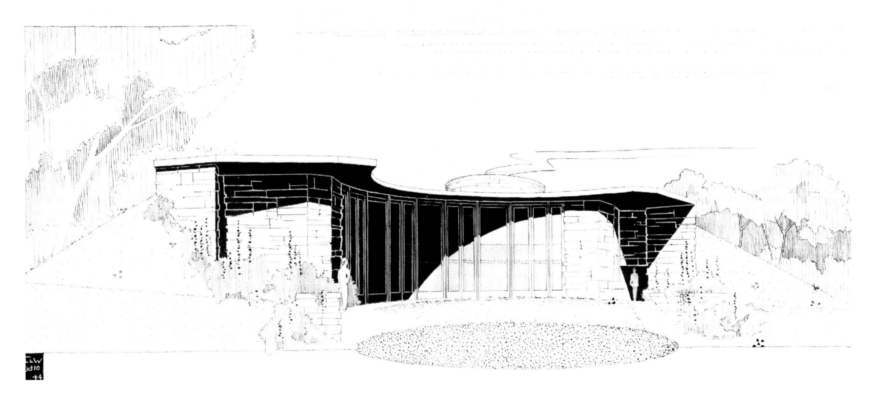

LEFT

FRANK LLOYD WRIGHT

Dining room.

FRANK LLOYD WRIGHT

Perspective view of the
Herbert A. Jacobs House,
1944. Ink and graphite on
paper. Gift of Herbert and
Katherine Jacobs.

HIGHWAYS OF THE FUTURE 1943

HUGH FERRISS

Promotional print for the Portland Cement Company

BRIDGE OVER CALDWELL AVENUE ca. 1947

JAMES EDWIN QUINN

CONGRESS STREET EXPRESSWAY 1945

JAMES EDWIN QUINN

From Congress Parkway to Oak Park Avenue

James Edwin Quinn designed high-style apartment buildings (see p. 80) until the Great Depression hit. After that, he worked for Cook County as a highway architect designing bridges and overpasses as part of the post–World War II creation of the Interstate Highway system throughout the United States. Among Quinn's papers are a series of promotional prints distributed during World War II by the Portland Cement Company which, through the dramatic drawings of renowned architectural renderer Hugh Ferriss, showed the world of the future. Although the American Interstate Highway system did not draw on those visions, it was, in part, catalyzed by the knowledge President Eisenhower gained of the German autobahn system while he headed the European Allies in World War II. Another factor was the need to quickly evacuate cities and move troops in the event of another global war. In real terms, however, these new highways led to rapid postwar suburbanization outside those cities.

ABOVE

HUGH FERRISS

Highways of the Future. Promotional print for the Portland Cement Company, 1943. Printed paper. Gift of James Edwin Quinn.

ABOVE RIGHT

JAMES EDWIN QUINN

Presentation photo of the bridge over Caldwell Avenue, ca. 1947. Hand-tinted photographic print on paper. Gift of James Edwin Quinn.

RIGHT

JAMES EDWIN QUINN

Aerial perspective of Congress Street Expressway, from Congress Parkway to Oak Park Avenue, del. Al Burnes, 1945. Graphite and printed paper mounted on board; ink, gouache, and watercolor added. Gift of James Edwin Quinn.

ILLINOIS INSTITUTE OF TECHNOLOGY 1955

LUDWIG MIES VAN DER ROHE

When Ludwig Mies van der Rohe moved to Chicago from Germany in 1938 he was fortunate to have had the Armour Institute of Technology (later Illinois Institute of Technology, or IIT) as his base of operation. Partly because of the hiatus in construction during the Great Depression and World War II, he was able to reshape the curriculum at the architecture school and train a new generation of architects to reform architecture and society through an apprecia-

LUDWIG MIES VAN DER ROHE

Presentation drawing of exterior view of Chapel and Parish House, ca. 1949–52. Graphite and charcoal on Strathmore board. Gift of A. James Speyer.

tion of minimal modernism. In the early 1940s Mies and his colleague in the architecture and planning department, Ludwig Hilberseimer, set out to plan a campus with structures that projected their attitude toward steel, brick, and glass. Their designs became even more skeletal and minimal when they were executed in the 1950s. The structures reflect a similar shift toward universality and openness in all of Mies's work in the United States.

ABOVE

LUDWIG MIES VAN DER ROHE

Chapel, Illinois Institute of
Technology

RIGHT

LUDWIG MIES VAN DER ROHE

Perspective sketch of interior
of Chapel, ca. 1949. Graphite
on paper. Gift of A. James Speyer.

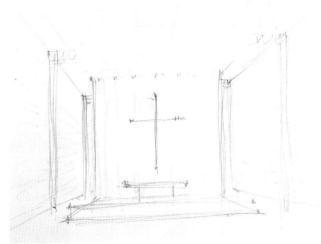

LEFT AND RIGHT

Ludwig Mies van der Rohe

Crown Hall, Illinois Institute of Technology.

BELOW

Perspective study of proposed Architecture Building, Illinois Institute of Technology, ca. 1944. Graphite, colored pencil, and charcoal on tracing paper. Restricted gift of the Auxiliary Board.

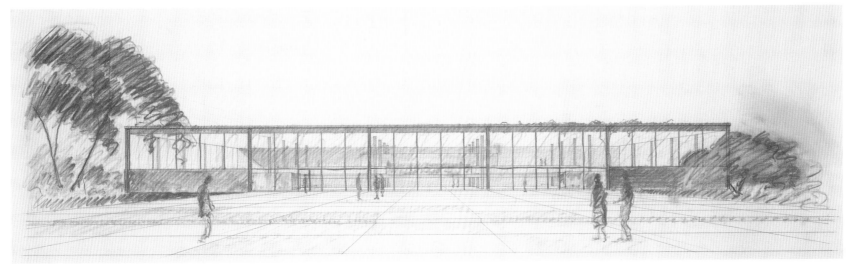

860–880 LAKE SHORE DRIVE 1950

LUDWIG MIES VAN DER ROHE

PACE Associates and Holsman, Holsman, Klekamp & Taylor, associate architects

Even before Mies finished his buildings at IIT he designed and constructed a series of important residential works, from the Farnsworth House in Plano, Illinois (1946–51), to Chicago apartment buildings such as the Promontory Apartments (1946–49) and 860–880 Lake Shore Drive (1948–51). These last two Lake Shore towers represent the epitome of Mies's skeletal steel and glass construction, setting the tone for his buildings to come. Like the Promontory Apartments, they were built for developer Herbert Greenwald, who, until his death in an airliner crash in 1959, was influential in providing Mies with major commissions, such as the Commonwealth Promenade Apartments (1953–56) and others as far away as Montreal. As on many of his other large-scale projects Mies worked with associate architects who, as in the case of Charles Genther of PACE Associates, were former students of his, thereby allowing him to maintain control over the execution of his design philosophy.

ABOVE

LUDWIG MIES VAN DER ROHE

Perspective sketch of high-rise buildings, possibly Promontory Apartments or 860–880 Lake Shore Drive, ca. 1946–48. Pencil on paper. Restricted gifts of the Architecture Society and the Alexander C. and Tillie S. Speyer Foundation in honor of John Zukowsky, and through prior gift of the Three Oaks Wrecking Company and Carson, Pirie Scott and Company; Samuel P. Avery Endowment and Edward E. Ayer Endowment in Memory of Charles L. Hutchinson.

FOLLOWING PAGES

LUDWIG MIES VAN DER ROHE

860–880 Lake Shore Drive seen from Lake Michigan (third and fourth in from right). The two black buildings to their right are 900–910 Lake Shore Drive, also by Mies van der Rohe.

RUTH FORD HOUSE 1950

BRUCE GOFF

404 South Edgelawn, Aurora, Illinois

During World War II Bruce Goff was a Seabee in the Navy, designing creative structures at Camp Parks, California, in 1944–45 for the Officers Club, Lounge and Star Bar, and Chapel. In those buildings—particularly the Chapel (moved in 1947 to nearby San Lorenzo as their Community Church), which was made from the ribs of a Quonset hut—Goff learned to shape a space from found materials, something that he later perfected in the Bavinger House (1950) in Norman, Oklahoma, which is built of rough stone and glass slag. A similarly important Chicago-area home from this era is the Ruth Ford House—a 1,700-square-foot residence that uses salvaged Quonset hut ribs, skylights made from plexiglass observation domes secured from surplus aircraft, and anthracite coal walls. The last was Goff's solution to the owner's request for black walls in her art studio.

BRUCE GOFF

Elevation of Ruth Ford House, 1947–49. Ink on tracing paper. Gift of Shin'enKan, Inc.

O'HARE INTERNATIONAL AIRPORT 1952

RALPH BURKE ASSOCIATES

Later additions: C.F. Murphy Associates

Orchard Field served as a Douglas Aircraft Company transport factory in World War II. After the war, the city of Chicago acquired the site and, in 1949, renamed the airport after Lt. Commander Edward "Butch" O'Hare, America's first ace in World War II. Chicago was already the air transport hub of the nation with its new terminal and facilities at Midway, but in its plans for O'Hare, the city determined that this new site, well away from Midway's urban location, would be ideal for future air travel expansion. Ralph Burke's firm planned the new airport and C.F. Murphy Associates designed the new terminals, which were officially dedicated by Mayor Richard J. Daley and President John F. Kennedy on March 23, 1963. The concrete, steel, and glass modernist buildings were among the first for the new jet age, incorporating the now ubiquitous jetways that connected the planes to their arrival gates. Since then, O'Hare grew for many years to become the world's busiest airport and, although it has, in part, ceded that title to Atlanta's Hartsfield International, it still handles more than 66 million passengers a year.

ABOVE

Original terminal at O'Hare International Airport (now demolished).

RIGHT

RALPH BURKE ASSOCIATES

Bird's-eye view of proposed master plan for O'Hare International Airport, del. William F. Kaiser, 1952. Watercolor, gouache, and crayon on illustration board. Gift of Ralph Burke Associates.

FOLLOWING PAGES

One of the terminals designed by C.F. Murphy Associates, 1963.

O'HARE MASTER PLAN-1952
RALPH BURKE ASSOCIATES

INLAND STEEL BUILDING 1958

WALTER A. NETSCH AND BRUCE J. GRAHAM

Skidmore, Owings & Merrill
30 West Monroe Street

Having done large-scale work for the U.S. government at Oak Ridge, Tennessee, among other sites, during World War II, the partnership of Louis Skidmore, Nathaniel Owings, and John Merrill—Skidmore, Owings & Merrill, or SOM—was poised to receive major commissions after the war. As touted in their marketing information of the time, the great strength of SOM was its variety of modern solutions rather than one universal answer imposed upon clients as in, say, the works of Mies and his followers. When the Inland Steel Building was first undertaken, Walter A. Netsch was the designer in charge, and his solution featured an all-glass, double-wall system. When Netsch was removed by Owings to work on the Air Force Academy in Colorado Springs (1954), Bruce J. Graham took over the job. Graham kept the plan, which separated the service core from the open office floors, but he clad the final building in stainless steel to emphasize the owner's corporate image. Graham's success on this building led him to other commercial jobs for SOM, culminating in his being the partner in charge for the famous Hancock (1970, see p. 140) and Sears (1974; left) towers in Chicago. Likewise, Netsch's work at the Air Force Academy, particularly his striking chapel (1963), led him to other institutional projects for the firm.

ABOVE

SKIDMORE, OWINGS & MERRILL

The Sears Tower, designed by Bruce J. Graham, with engineer Fazlur Khan. The Inland Steel Building is in front of the Sears Tower.

RIGHT

Inland Steel Building.

FAR RIGHT TOP

SKIDMORE, OWINGS & MERRILL

Preliminary model for the Inland Steel Building, ca. 1954, designed by Walter A. Netsch. Plexiglass and enameled steel. Gift of Walter A. Netsch.

FAR RIGHT BOTTOM

Final model for the Inland Steel Building, ca. 1954–55, designed by Bruce J. Graham. Mixed media. Gift of Ryerson Tull Inc., Chicago.

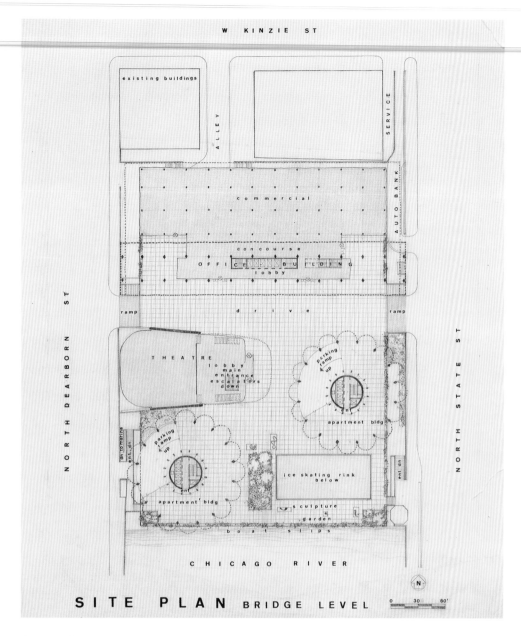

SITE PLAN BRIDGE LEVEL

W KINZIE ST

existing buildings

ALLEY

SERVICE

AUTO BANK

commercial

concourse

OFFICE BUILDING
lobby

NORTH DEARBORN ST

ramp   d r i v e   ramp

THEATRE
lobby
main
entrance
escalators
down

NORTH STATE ST

parking
ramp
up

ent.

apartment bldg

parking
ramp
up

ent. dn

marine

ent.

ice skating rink
below

ent. dn

apartment bldg

sculpture
garden

b o a t   s l i p s

CHICAGO RIVER

N

0   30   60'

BERTRAND GOLDBERG ASSOCIATES

Site plan for Marina City, n.d.
Graphite, print, and zip-a-tone
on vellum. The Archive of
Bertrand Goldberg, gifted by his
children through his estate.

RIGHT

Marina City with office building and theater (now House
of Blues) in front.

MARINA CITY 1965

BERTRAND GOLDBERG ASSOCIATES

300 North Street

The twin towers of Marina City, located on Chicago's riverfront, are among the most photographed of all the city's landmarks. The complex consists of two towers for parking and apartments, an adjacent slab-like office tower, and an irregularly shaped theater. Architect Bertrand Goldberg advocated high-density urban living as an alternative to the exodus to the suburbs. He supported the idea of a "city within a city" that would contain all the amenities necessary for the residents, while making the most rational use of expensive urban land.

The 60-story circular towers (each with 21 stories of parking below the residential units) were for a time the tallest reinforced-concrete structures in the world. At that time, they were considered innovative not only for their expressive form, but also for their construction. The cores were erected first and then served as cranes as the floors were attached one by one from bottom to top. The resulting 900 apartments, 450 units in each building, are wedge-shaped. Apartments range from studios to two-bedroom units, but all have their own balcony.

A low building for recreational amenities such as a bowling alley and pool connects the other buildings of the complex. The structure situated between the offices and towers was designed to house theaters (today it is home to the House of Blues). Its impressive roofline is formed by sprayed concrete slung on steel catenary cables supported by a curving frame.

CHICAGO CIVIC CENTER
(RICHARD J. DALEY CENTER) 1965

JACQUES BROWNSON

C.F. Murphy Associates
Loebel Schlossman & Bennett and Skidmore, Owings & Merrill,
associate architects
Washington, Randolph, Dearborn, and Clark Streets

Within the framework of a program to encourage growth and ultimately support the tax base of the city, the Central Area Committee, a coalition of civic organizations, public agencies, and private business, founded in 1956, put forward plans and proposals to encourage the vitality of the city's center. The new building, housing many courtrooms and offices for the city, county, and state, was completed in 1965 and expressed the way of the future.

In 1960 C.F. Murphy, under lead designer Jacques Brownson, was selected from a field of nineteen firms that submitted proposals for this commission. As originally proposed, the plan called for two glass and steel buildings slightly over 20 stories each. However, a single tower proved to be the most economical and efficient way to meet the program needs. The Mies-inspired modern building, more closely resembling an office building than one for government functions, was built of Cor-Ten steel using a modular system. Rising 31 stories and almost 650 feet, it was for a time the tallest in the city.

Because the tower occupied only 35 percent of the site, a vast urban plaza was created. Discussions were held about elements to be included in the plaza, and a sculpture seemed essential. Works by Henry Moore and Maillol were proposed, but the final decision was for Pablo Picasso. In 1966, with the installation of a specially commissioned monumental sculpture by Picasso, also made of Cor-Ten steel, the composition of tower and plaza became more balanced and inviting.

FOLLOWING PAGES

C.F. MURPHY ASSOCIATES

Perspective view of plaza at Chicago Civic Center (Richard J. Daley Center), 1963. Watercolor and gouache on board. Gift of Helmut Jahn.

Francill

TIME-LIFE BUILDING 1966

HARRY WEESE AND ASSOCIATES

541 North Fairbanks Court

Harry Weese was one of Chicago's great individualist architects, following in the tradition, in some ways, of people such as Louis Sullivan, Frank Lloyd Wright, and Bruce Goff. Part of Weese's individual approach to modernism came from his training at the Cranbrook Academy of Arts, a school long associated with the personalized modernism of the father-and-son team of Eliel and Eero Saarinen. Thus, Weese buildings were often designed specifically for the needs of each client, and they all look very different from each other. These range from his First Baptist Church in Columbus, Indiana (1965), which merges a brick medieval monastery with a country church, to the Washington, D.C., Metro System (1966 and later), complete with grand, coffered barrel vaults to recall the great railroad stations of the past, to the William J. Campbell Courthouse Annex in Chicago (1975), an angular skyscraper prison of concrete with five-inch-wide window slits for the inmates' cells.

His skyscraper for Time-Life's subscription services division is a high-rise of Cor-Ten steel whose bronze mirrored-glass surfaces distinguish it from an orthodox Miesian skyscraper. The building's double-deck elevators were a first for the industry.

HARRY WEESE AND ASSOCIATES

Perspective view of the Time-Life Building, del. Robert E. Bell, 1966. Graphite and marker on yellow tracing paper. Gift of Robert E. Bell.

SEVENTEENTH CHURCH OF CHRIST SCIENTIST 1968

HARRY WEESE AND ASSOCIATES

35 East Wacker Drive

Harry Weese's curved Christian Science church is situated at a dramatic interchange next to the Chicago River and recalls the tradition of centrally planned classicist churches for that religion.

RIGHT

HARRY WEESE AND ASSOCIATES

Exterior perspective study for the Seventeenth Church of Christ Scientist, ca. 1968. Pencil on tracing paper. Gift of Harry Weese and Associates.

ABRAHAM LINCOLN OASIS, TRI-STATE TOLLWAY 1968

DAVID HAID & ASSOCIATES
South Holland, Illinois

When people think of roadside architecture they immediately think of fast-food chains, especially McDonald's and its parabolic arches and signage of the 1950s, which were first developed in Chicago's suburbs. But Illinois Tollways have another architectural form from the 1950s and 1960s when it comes to roadside eateries. Many are modernist structures designed by Charles Genther, a Mies student who was the partner in charge of PACE Associates, that bridge the highway. These restaurants were operated as Fred Harvey restaurants, a Chicago-based chain whose earlier eateries along the Santa Fe railroad lines gained the public's imagination through the feature film *The Harvey Girls* (1946), starring Judy Garland, Angela Lansbury, and Cyd Charisse. Perhaps the most elegant eatery along the toll road system was that designed by David Haid, another Mies student, in South Holland. Its skeletal steel and glass structure and big picture windows enabled diners to see the exciting advance of cross-country driving unfold beneath them.

Reconstruction of first McDonald's originally built in 1955.

BOTTOM RIGHT

DAVID HAID & ASSOCIATES

Elevation study for the Abraham Lincoln Oasis, Tri-State Tollway, 1965–67. Pencil, conte, and charcoal on paper. Gift of David Haid.

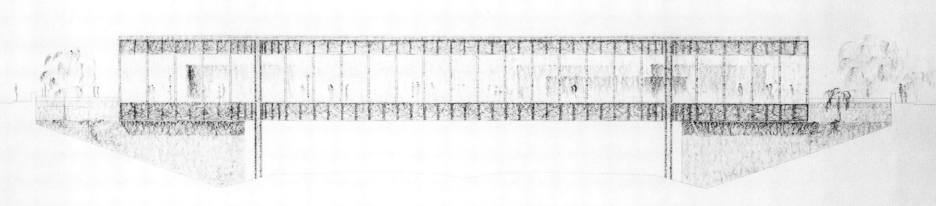

FIRST NATIONAL BANK BUILDING 1969

C.F. MURPHY ASSOCIATES WITH PERKINS & WILL

One First National Plaza

On a site in the center of the Loop, zoning ordinances of 1964 allowed a 60-story skyscraper with an area of over 4 million square feet. First National Bank commissioned two collaborating firms to undertake such a design: C.F. Murphy Associates with Stanley Gladych, Carter H. Manny Jr., and Charles Rummel heading their design team; and the Perkins & Will Partnership with Lawrence Perkins, Philip Will, and Charles William Brubaker as designers. Drawings done by Brubaker during meetings serve as "visual minutes" of those meetings and a record of the design process. Early design schemes showed the prominence of the bank building in an emblematic corridor in the Loop that extended from Federal Center to the Civic Center. Initial plans included a transmitting tower, which would have made the structure the city's tallest, but it was later omitted and the final building is only 850 feet tall.

Even the earliest sketches indicate a building wider at the bottom than at the top. The tapering toward the top responded, in part, to the need for large publicly accessible spaces at the lower levels and for smaller floor plates with more light for the tenant-occupied offices above. The exterior cladding of the building was, however, a subject of debate. Perkins & Will planned to use contrasting light and dark tones, but the monochromatic proposal of the C.F. Murphy firm prevailed.

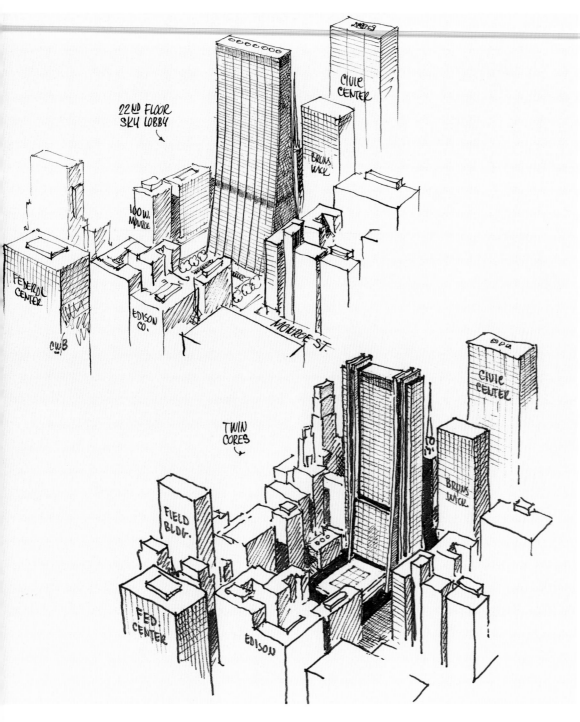

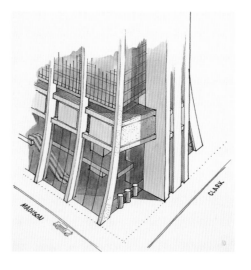

C.F. MURPHY ASSOCIATES WITH PERKINS & WILL

Perspective studies for First National Bank Building, 1964–66. Black ink with brown wash on notebook paper. Gift of C. William Brubaker.

C.F. MURPHY ASSOCIATES WITH PERKINS & WILL

Perspective study of entrance at Clark and Madison Streets, del. C. William Brubaker. Black ink with brown wash on notebook paper. Gift of C. William Brubaker.

McCormick Place 1971

GENE SUMMERS

C.F. Murphy Associates
East 23rd Street and South Lake Shore Drive

In 1953–54 Mies van der Rohe prepared a spectacular convention center project with a grand, open central space for the South Side Planning Board. Without a specific location, the project was intended to prompt the city and state to seriously consider building such a facility. This led to the commissioning of a convention center on the lakefront at 23rd Street that was designed by Alfred Shaw (see pp.86–87 for his Field Building) and built in 1960 as the world's largest exposition hall. It was then destroyed in a fire on January 16, 1967. Its replace-

ment, McCormick Place, opened in 1971. Designed by Gene Summers, who studied with and worked for Mies, it is a dramatic steel and glass structure with a cantilevered roof and a spacious convention and trade fair space within that is, in sprit, the descendant of Mies's design. In an effort to maintain Chicago's status as the most important convention city in the country, later additions to the exhibition hall complex were made by Skidmore, Owings & Merrill (1986) and Thompson Ventulett Stainback & Associates (1996), but neither is as elegant as Summers's original building.

LEFT

McCormick Place before the fire of 1967.

ABOVE

C.F. MURPHY ASSOCIATES

Presentation drawing for McCormick Place, del. Helmut Jacoby, 1969. Ink, graphite, and watercolor on board.
Gift of Helmut Jahn.

RIGHT

Perspective view of McCormick Place, ca. 1967, published in *Architectural Record*, May 1971. Photocollage on board.
Gift of Helmut Jahn.

JOHN HANCOCK CENTER 1970

BRUCE GRAHAM AND FAZLUR KHAN

Skidmore, Owings & Merrill
875 North Michigan Avenue

With the construction of the John Hancock Center for offices, residences, parking, and commercial space, the North Michigan Avenue area began a transformation based on mixed-use high-rises that extended through the 1990s. The 100-story, 1,127-foot-tall (1,145 feet to the top of the antenna) Hancock Tower, designed under partner Bruce Graham and engineer Fazlur Khan of Skidmore, Owings & Merrill, has a tapering form and striking cross braces that contribute to its monumental presence. It served as a beacon, leading the way for development on the avenue. Upscale residential and retail centers effectively formed a new leading shopping district, taking away that traditional retail role from the department stores and other establishments located on and around State Street in the Loop.

To call attention to the reinvention of the Chicago skyline, the Chicago Architectural Club sponsored a public design competition, "TOPS." Architects were encouraged to propose alterations to the tops of actual buildings through a no-holds-barred process of addition, subtraction, abstraction, or invention. The Hancock Center was a perfect candidate for Peggy Smolka's reimagining.

PEGGY SMOLKA WOLFF

Chicago Architectural Club's TOPS Competition Entry: John Hancock Center, 1983. Mixed media, including ink and graphite on polyester film.
Gift of Peggy Smolka Wolff.

WATER TOWER PLACE 1976

LOEBL SCHLOSSMAN BENNETT & DART
(Loebl Schlossman Dart and Hackl)
with C.F. Murphy Associates
845 North Michigan Avenue

Following the Hancock building's lead, other mixed-use high-rises were constructed in the area. First was Water Tower Place in 1976 by Loebl Schlossman Bennett & Dart, followed by One Magnificent Mile (1983) and a Neiman Marcus department store (1983) topped by the Olympia Center's tower (1986), all by Skidmore, Owings & Merrill. A multiuse development at 900 North Michigan Avenue (1989) was undertaken by the New York firm of Kohn Pedersen & Fox. A condominium tower of Chicago Place at 700 North Michigan designed by Solomon Cordwell Buenz, and City Place by Loebl, Schlossman & Hackl at 676 North Michigan Avenue were both completed in 1990.

Water Tower Place, composed of a 12-story base and a 62-story tower, continues to be one of the most successful multiuse complexes on North Michigan. Inside, spaces for retail, offices, and leisure activities coexist with a 400-room hotel and 260 luxury residences.

The seven-level shopping complex is constructed around a great atrium that is 60 feet wide at the fifth floor and narrows asymmetrically above and below that point. A four-lane motor concourse, running through the building from Pearson to Chestnut Streets, separates the commercial area from the condominium and hotel lobbies.

The uniform size and placement of the tower's windows give the light gray marble building an understated appearance. The original unadorned marble of the base building was altered during a major renovation by the California office of the firm of Wimberly Allison Tong & Goo, completed in 2002. The designers added dramatic exterior lighting and glass cylinders at the two Michigan Avenue corners to gain more retail display areas. They attached stainless steel fins to the facade to update its look. They also revamped the Michigan Avenue lobby, and the original cascading waterfall (by Warren Platner Associates of New Haven, Connecticut) was redesigned by Wetdesign of California with small bursts of water creating kinetic patterns.

LEFT

John Hancock Center (left) and Water Tower Place (right).

RIGHT

LOEBL, SCHLOSSMAN, BENNETT & DART

Preliminary study for Water Tower Place Proposal, del. Wojciech Madeyski, 1970. Pencil and felt-tip marking pen on white paper. Gift of Helmut Jahn.

THE TITANIC 1978

STANLEY TIGERMAN

Stanley Tigerman created this fanciful collage of Mies's Crown Hall, the Illinois Institute of Technology building that houses the School of Architecture (see p. 108), sinking into Lake Michigan. The work makes a strong statement about the end of modernism in Chicago after the 1969 death of Mies van der Rohe. Indeed, the mid to late 1970s witnessed similar critiques of the modern movement throughout the nation and the world. Interest in elaborate architectural drawings and in ornamentation and historic contextualism for buildings increased throughout the 1980s. These factors were aided by the Bicentennial of the United States (1976), which celebrated all things historic, and the renderings in the Museum of Modern Art's landmark exhibition *The Architecture of the Ecole des Beaux Arts* (1977). In Chicago, Stanley Tigerman made varied and extensive contributions to the dialogue about architecture. He was one of the curators of important exhibitions that stressed a new pluralism of design, such as *Chicago Architects* (1976) and *Late Entries to the Chicago Tribune Competition* (1980), and he participated in the landmark exhibit *Seven Chicago Architects* (1976–77), the beginnings of the so-called Chicago Seven group of architects. The last grew into the popular Chicago Architectural Club (founded 1979), named after a historic architects' club from a century before.

STANLEY TIGERMAN

The Titanic, 1978.
Photomontage on paper.
Gift of Stanley Tigerman.

ILLINOIS REGIONAL LIBRARY FOR THE BLIND AND PHYSICALLY HANDICAPPED 1978

STANLEY TIGERMAN & ASSOCIATES

Roosevelt and Blue Island Avenues

Located on a small triangular site west of Chicago's Loop, the Illinois Regional Library for the Blind and Physically Handicapped was designed to support three main functions: a library for the blind and wheelchair bound, a branch library for the local community, and a distribution center for specialized materials. The brightly colored structure is triangular and hugs the street on two sides.

Currently, the library functions have moved to other facilities and the building's future and alternative uses are under discussion. Inside, the original library for the blind and wheelchair bound was located on the main floor. A 165-foot-long corridor was the main organizing feature. It extended along the perimeter walls of the building. A built-in counter along the corridor provided a constant reference for visitors, much in the way a handrail would. The linear quality and built-in furniture were easy to memorize by blind patrons.

Tigerman created a building that while serving its constituencies also had his desired combination of "spirit, wit, and informality."

STANLEY TIGERMAN & ASSOCIATES

Presentation drawing for main floor plan for Illinois Library for the Blind and Physically Handicapped, ca. 1978. Graphite and colored pencil on white vellum-finish tracing paper. Gift of Stanley Tigerman, Tigerman McCurry Architects.

RIGHT

Main-floor library with built-in serpentine counter.

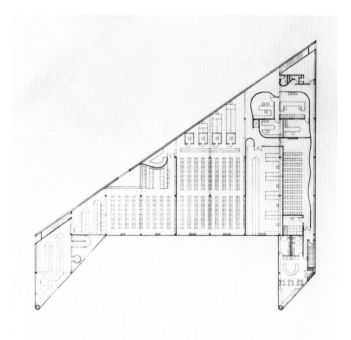

LATE ENTRIES TO THE CHICAGO TRIBUNE TOWER COMPETITION 1980

The 1980 exhibition *Late Entries to the Chicago Tribune Tower Competition*, curated by Stanley Tigerman and Stuart Cohen, was an extension of the exhibitions showing work of the "Chicago Seven," a group of architects established in the 1970s that pushed the envelope of architectural thought and theory in Chicago. The opportunity to revisit the Tribune Tower competition almost sixty years after the original brought in 60 submissions by invited architects. In their proposals national and international architects reconsidered some of the ideas in the 1922 competition that resulted in the tower by Howells & Hood (see pp. 66–67).

Robert A.M. Stern's idea was based on the original entry by Adolf Loos, who designed a building in the shape of a Doric column. While Loos's proposal contradicted his modern stance against ornamentation, Stern's postmodern design is firmly based in his own beliefs in using historical vocabularies for contemporary projects. Stern's 1980 design reshapes Loos's original idea into a buildable, and therefore marketable, product. He creates a pilaster "to retain the shape of the standard office building" and greatly exaggerates the three elements of base, shaft, and capital. He then pays homage to Mies by using modern technology and materials, glass and steel, for the proposed construction.

ROBERT A.M. STERN

Perspective elevation for Late Entry to the Chicago Tribune Tower Competition.
Airbrushed ink on illustration board. Restricted gift of Mr. and Mrs. Thomas J. Eyerman; Mr. and Mrs David Hilliard; Mrs. Irving F. Stein Sir., in memory of B. Leo Steif; and Mr. and Mrs. Ben Weese.

A second entry that has become part of the permanent collection of the Art Institute is by Charles Moore of the California firm of Moore-Ruble-Yudell. It refers to the much-acclaimed second-place entry to the original competition, by Eliel Saarinen. Moore has taken the original submission, broken apart its facade and inserted a Piranesian glass iceberg. The text accompanying Moore's submission is an excerpt from Louis Sullivan's commentary on Saarinen's original design. Sullivan elegized the project as "qualifying . . . in every technical regard . . . it goes freely in advance, and displays a high science of design such as the world up to this day had neither known or surmised." Charles Moore seemed to agree.

CHARLES W. MOORE WITH JOHN RUBLE AND BUZZ YUDELL

Presentation drawing for Late Entry to the Chicago Tribune Tower Competition. Colored pencil on "vellum" tracing paper. Architecture Fellows Restricted Gift.

McDonald's Floating Restaurant 1983

SITE (SCULPTURE IN THE ENVIRONMENT, INC.)

Berwyn, Illinois

The McDonald's corporation's hometown called for a special design by SITE, architects known for blurring the boundaries between public art and architecture. The first step in their process was to understand the design of standard McDonald's facilities by thinking of them as a kit of parts. Mansard roofs, colonial-style windows, brick-faced exterior walls, and the golden arches are commonly used as symbols and are easily recognized by the general public. In Berwyn, the architectural elements are dislodged from their usual positions, and from the exterior, the structure seems to "float" in space. The brick walls do not rest on the ground. The roof also appears separated from the walls; lighting under the roof heightens this illusion at night. An "under-the-building" garden further transforms conventional elements into something unexpected. The McDonald's design was the continuation of the floating wall idea SITE first used in 1982 in a residence on the top two floors of a New York building.

McDonald's Restaurant – Chicago

SITE J.W. 1986

SITE (SCULPTURE IN THE ENVIRONMENT, INC.)

Perspective sketches for McDonald's Floating Restaurant, del. James Wines, 1982–83. Ink line and wash on paper. Through prior gifts of Three Oaks Wrecking Company.

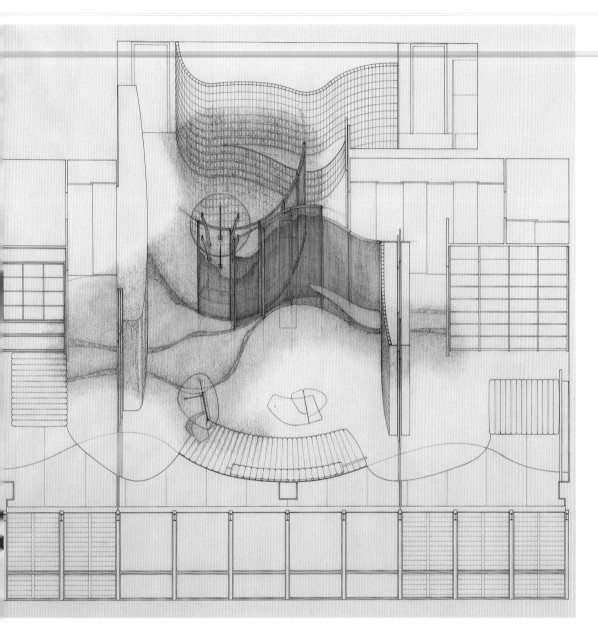

PAINTED APARTMENT 1983

KRUECK & OLSEN ARCHITECTS
(now Krueck & Sexton Architects)
2400 North Lakeview Avenue

This apartment on the north side of Chicago overlooks Lincoln Park and Lake Michigan. Located in a high-rise designed by Mies van der Rohe, it was originally a three-bedroom apartment. The owner sought to change it from an apartment that displayed art to an apartment that was itself an artistic composition. Concepts and concerns of the architects such as transparency, materials, textures, and the layering of space are patent in all parts of this project.

The architects eliminated all interior walls, except those enclosing the kitchen and bathroom. The exterior window wall, as is usual in a Mies building, extended from floor to ceiling. Now, a low stainless steel platform extends the length of the window wall, curving in and out to accommodate furniture and ease movement in the space. Glass-block walls illuminated from within, sliding panels, and wardrobes define the living space. These elements are finished with highly metallic automobile paints. The central area is manipulated by perforated metal screens of varied densities. The project is titled the "Painted Apartment" for the seven shades of gray and three accent colors that are used on floors, ceilings, and perimeter walls.

KRUECK & OLSEN ARCHITECTS

Axonometric (above) and perspective (right) views of the Painted Apartment, 1983. Black and colored ink on paper (axonometric) and photo enlargement (perspective). Gift of Krueck & Olsen Architects.

CHICAGO BOARD OF TRADE 1981

HELMUT JAHN

C.F. Murphy Associates
141 W. Jackson Boulevard

In the mid-1980s, architect Helmut Jahn became well known for designing prominent buildings both in the United States and abroad. Respected architecture publications and books focused on his work. He was talked about in fashion and society magazines and well as in *Newsweek* and *Time*. His work combined history and context, gave symbolic elements a new interpretation, and employed new materials. His architecture was a union of postmodernism and high-tech.

Chicago in the 1980s looked to Jahn and his firm, C.F. Murphy Associates, for several buildings, including an addition to the Board of Trade in 1981. The program called for support spaces for the trading floor and offices for the exchange members. The new addition, clad in black and silver glass, is adjacent to the existing Board of Trade. Its roofline echoes that of the old. The vertical strips of windows and the massing of the new building also pay homage to the Art Deco style of its predecessor. Its 12th-story office atrium, with cascading curvilinear glass walls, is based on a similar design in the original building.

ABOVE LEFT

C.F. MURPHY ARCHITECTS

12th-story atrium.

LEFT

Two design studies of elevations for Chicago Board of Trade addition, ca. 1980. Colored ink on white tracing paper. Gift of Helmut Jahn.

RIGHT

Top of the Board of Trade seen from the roof of the LaSalle Street train station, with original Board of Trade, designed by Holabird & Root in 1929–30, behind.

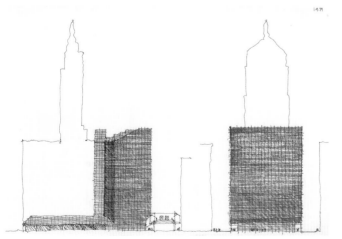

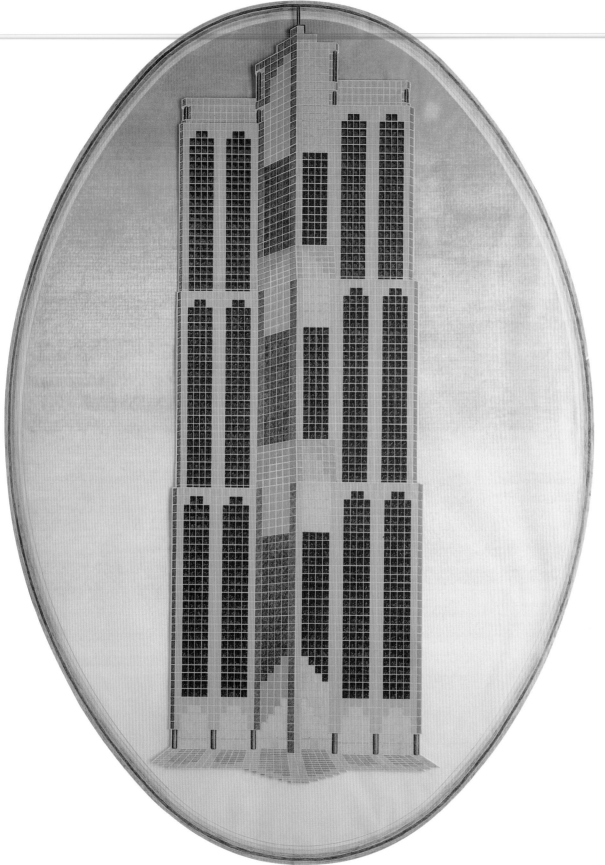

ONE SOUTH WACKER DRIVE 1982

HELMUT JAHN

C.F. Murphy Associates

The speculative office tower at One South Wacker was completed in 1982. The 40-story building is composed of three sections, each of which steps back as the building rises. The two-toned glass envelope features dark vertical bands that reinforce the tower's height and reduce its bulk. A two-story lobby connects the Wacker Drive and Madison Street entrances, and its polished stone walls and the patterning of its fluorescent lights, evoke the Art Deco.

C.F. MURPHY ASSOCIATES

Elevation of One South Wacker Drive, 1981, del. Helmut Jahn. Colored pencil and silver tape on paper. Gift of Helmut Jahn.

RIGHT

One South Wacker by Helmut Jahn and assisted by James Goettsch with Sears Tower seen to right.

James R. Thompson Center 1985

HELMUT JAHN

Murphy/Jahn Architects
With Lester B. Knight and Associates
Randolph, LaSalle, Lake, and Clark Streets

One of the most daring buildings of Chicago's Loop is the James R. Thompson Center (originally named the State of Illinois Center) by Helmut Jahn. Commissioned by then-governor James R. Thompson and completed in 1985, this building created a new symbolic landmark for the city. It is located directly north of City Hall and County Building and diagonally opposite the Civic Center (see p. 126) by Jahn's predecessor firm of C.F. Murphy and Associates. But, it also had to respond to the functional necessities of the government offices and services housed within and the required commercial spaces at street and lower levels. The building lines the street where the El travels, while a curved facade, toward Randolph and Clark Streets, deviates from the city's grid. It creates a generous urban plaza on the city side, which is an extension of the interior public plaza of the interior atrium.

In the State of Illinois building Helmut Jahn continued to experiment with "synthesizing" historical references with modern-day materials to create buildings that serve the present and future. The beveled glass cylinder protruding above the building mass is a nod to domed government buildings of the past, particularly state capitols. Inside is a spectacular, 17-story atrium with glass-walled elevators. Opaque and transparent glazing creates both various levels of transparency and the vertical rhythm of the outer skin. The building's visual clarity and openness represent the ideal qualities of effective government. The overall color scheme—a variation of red, white, and blue—lends symbolism, but also vibrancy, to the complex.

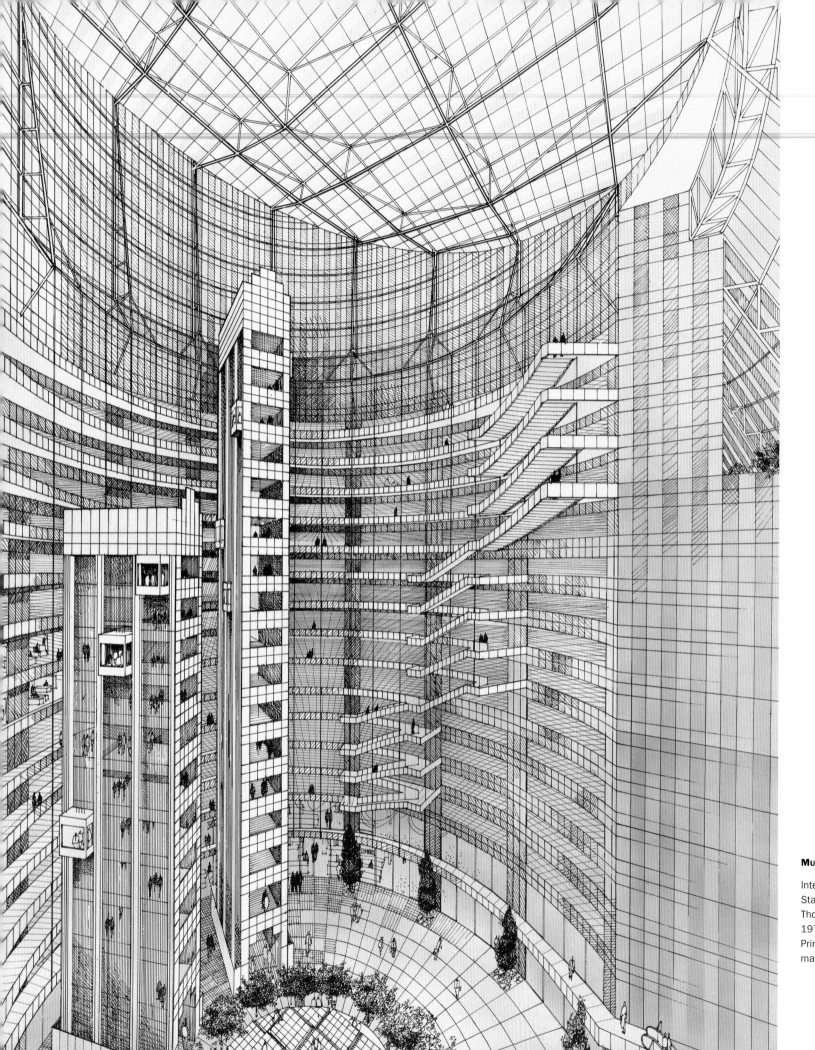

MURPHY/JAHN ARCHITECTS

Interior perspective view of State of Illinois (James R. Thompson) Center, ca. 1979–85, by Helmut Jahn. Print on paper pasted on masonite. Gift of Helmut Jahn.

Murphy/Jahn Architects

Axonometric rendering of the
Chicago and Northwestern
Terminal Building, del.
Michael Budilovsky, 1982.
Airbrushed ink on resin-coated
paper. Anonymous gift.

CHICAGO AND NORTHWESTERN TERMINAL BUILDING 1987

HELMUT JAHN

Murphy/Jahn Architects
500 West Madison Street

The Chicago and Northwestern Terminal Building at Madison and Canal Streets opened to the public in 1987. The office tower is located on top of the commuter train station. The building, with its oversized arched entry, likened to the grand portico of Louis Sullivan's Transportation Building of the 1893 World's Columbian Exposition, forms a gateway to and from the city. The east and west facades are relatively simple compared to the more sculptural forms of those facing north and south. The streamlined curves create a scalloped shape symbolic of trains and machine-made objects. Once again, designer Helmut Jahn used a sleek glass skin to create a glistening new landmark.

UNITED AIRLINES TERMINAL ONE 1987

HELMUT JAHN

Murphy/Jahn Architects
O'Hare International Airport

Within an overall master plan to expand, improve, and modernize O'Hare airport, the United Airlines Terminal was an outstanding contribution. Completed in 1987 and one of Helmut Jahn's professional high points of the decade, the building successfully combines and resolves issues of function, technology, and travelers' needs.

The terminal is composed of two parallel concourses with soaring glass barrel vaults, each 1,600 feet long. Connecting the two is an underground tunnel with moving sidewalks. The separation of concourses allows for the dual taxiing of wide-bodied aircraft on the tarmac above. One building doubles as a landside and airside terminal with the ticketing concourse on the upper level

MURPHY/JAHN ARCHITECTS

Interior perspective of United Airlines Terminal One, del. Rael Slutsky, 1987. Ink, graphite, and colored pencil on paper. Gift of Helmut Jahn.

FOLLOWING PAGES

Underground tunnel connecting Concourses B and C of United Airlines Terminal One.

and baggage claim area on the lower. Vehicles can approach the building at either level. The very large complex, over a million square feet, with gates for forty-two planes and a seemingly endless bank of counters in the ticketing pavilion, is extremely user-friendly. Jahn has accomplished this through the extensive use of natural light, careful detailing, and industrial yet elegant materials and colors. A prime example is the underground passageway. Undulating translucent glass walls, which are backlit, and a luminous ceiling with lines of light and color guide the user. A computer-generated pattern of moving lights and music further enhances the experience.

190 SOUTH LaSALLE STREET 1987

JOHN BURGEE ARCHITECTS WITH PHILIP JOHNSON

Shaw and Associates, associate architects

Architect John Burgee, a native Chicagoan, and Philip Johnson were partners with a New York–based firm from 1967 to 1987. This 40-story office tower was their first building in Chicago. After the success of Johnson's AT&T Building in New York (1980) with its exaggerated Chippendale roofline, the architects relied on overt historical references to create a striking image for their Chicago design. The gabled roofline, in this case, was inspired by a combination of sources both local and international. The architects looked to the Rookery Building of 1888 by Burnham and Root (see p. 32), the Masonic Temple of 1892 (demolished in 1939), and even Dutch Renaissance architecture with its ornate gables. The five-story base is clad in red granite, with the shaft in a lighter tone. Even more lavish and colorful is the lobby, 180 feet long and 40 feet wide, whose marble walls and pilasters support a gold-leaf barrel vault. The black and white marble floor with rose patterns makes for an impressive entrance and sets the tone for the rest of the building. Johnson took great pride in the lobby, calling it the "most lengthy, high and dignified lobby in the city."

LEFT

JOHN BURGEE WITH PHILIP JOHNSON

Preliminary lobby sketch for 190 South LaSalle Street, ca. 1983–86. Graphite and colored pencil on paper.
Gift of the John Buck Company.

RIGHT

JOHN BURGEE WITH PHILIP JOHNSON

Gable of main elevation, facing South LaSalle Street.

LEFT

**JOHN BURGEE WITH
PHILIP JOHNSON**

Preliminary lobby model for
190 South LaSalle Street,
ca. 1983–86. Gift of the
John Buck Company.

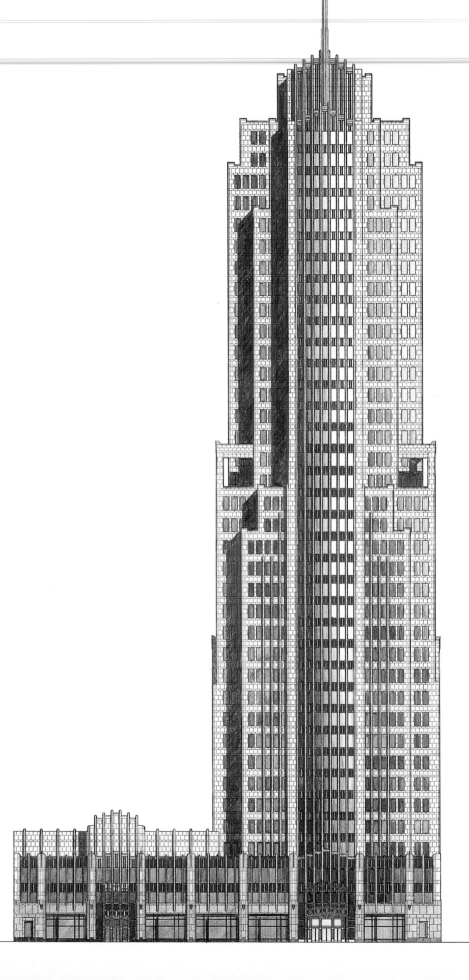

NBC TOWER 1989

ADRIAN SMITH

Skidmore, Owings & Merrill
454 North Columbus Drive

The NBC Tower was the second project to be completed in the Cityfront Center area, a 60-acre site bordered by the Chicago River, Lake Shore Drive, Grand Avenue, and Michigan Avenue. The overall planning for the site, a Planned Unit Development (PUD), set forth guidelines for the area that integrated commercial and residential uses; the guidelines were accepted in 1985.

The skyscraper is carefully sited near the neighboring Chicago Tribune Tower. It has a pedestrian plaza in front and a four-story building adjoined to the north. The lower structure provides television studios for NBC productions and the tower contains office space.

The NBC Tower design, by design partner Adrian Smith and studio heads John S. Burcher and Leonard Claggett of Skidmore, Owings & Merrill, pays homage to the great skyscrapers of the twentieth century. It is reminiscent of the RCA Building at Rockefeller Center in New York City (1931–40), the headquarters of NBC, and of the Chicago Tribune Tower—both landmark examples of Raymond Hood's architecture. The tower is clad in limestone. The multiple setbacks that the building incorporates and the tall spire on top are traditional architectural elements. The hint of flying buttresses nods to the nearby Tribune Tower. The sleekness and verticality of the NBC Tower is further accentuated on the Michigan Avenue facade by continuous vertical lines that extend from the base to the top.

SKIDMORE, OWINGS & MERRILL

Study for the NBC Corporate Center, 1986. Colored pencil on paper. Gift of Stanley Freehling.

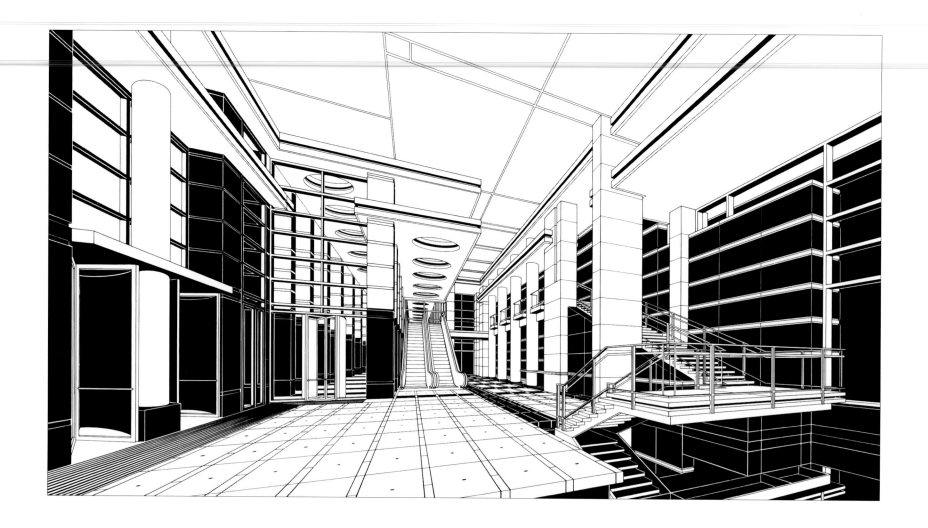

MORTON INTERNATIONAL BUILDING 1990

RALPH JOHNSON

Perkins & Will
100 North Riverside Plaza

A 36-story high-rise, the Morton International Building, is located on the river's edge in the west Loop area of the city. The architects took advantage of the location to create a two-level riverwalk and a small park. The challenging site, over a railroad yard, led to the definition of the cantilevered suspension truss to compensate for unusual foundation conditions at the southwest part of the site.

The two main materials used are pale granite and glass. Architect and designer Ralph Johnson successfully meshes the substantial (a solid building anchored to the

PERKINS & WILL

Lobby rendering of the Morton International Building, 1988–89, del. Ralph Johnson. Ink on mylar. Gift of Ralph Johnson.

ground) with lightness (conveyed by large, transparent glass areas). The massing consists of a series of simple stacked rectilinear blocks, each housing individual functions. Within a language of sleek modernism, certain elements lend a bit of nostalga: the suspension truss and the entrance canopy recall the industrial bridges along the river. The soaring clock tower that crowns the building pays homage to many historic skyscrapers in Chicago. In 2001 the majority of the building was leased to the Boeing Company, who added their company logo to the top of the building.

AMERICAN MEDICAL ASSOCIATION 1990

KENZO TANGE

Shaw & Associates, associate architects
515 North State Street

Internationally acclaimed Japanese architect and Pritzker Prize–winner Kenzo Tange designed his first Chicago skyscraper, a 30-story office building for the American Medical Association (AMA), in the 1980s. This was, however, his second commission in Chicago. He had previously undertaken a block-long riverfront park in Chicago's downtown near Dearborn Street. The new AMA building, completed in 1990, was one of the first large office towers to be built in the River North area. Unabashedly modern in materials and form, the building has a smooth skin of granite along with a glass and aluminum curtain wall. Horizontal bands formed by the changes in materials and color create the pattern of the building's envelope. The base of the structure and entrance are finished in white-flecked granite. The building's striking geometric shape resembles a ship's prow, with a distinctive four-story cutout near the top. Three facades run parallel to the streets while the southern facade is angled to form the point of the prow. This irregular form creates a striking image when approached from the south. The main entrance to the lobby protrudes from this prow.

Tange placed the building to the north side of the site to allow for the development of a future, smaller residential tower next door. The remaining space on the south side of the site was used to create an urban plaza. The plaza is not flat but formed by slightly undulating changes in the landscape and is dotted with trees. Steps on the eastern part provide access to Wabash Street, which is at a slightly higher level.

RIGHT

KENZO TANGE

Study model for the American Medical Association, 1988. Reflective plexiglass with applied tape collage and foam backing. Gift of Patrick Shaw, Shaw & Associates.

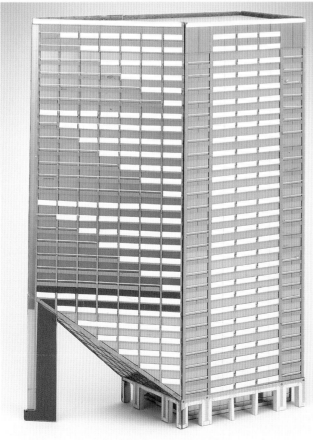

CRATE AND BARREL STORE 1990

SOLOMON CORDWELL BUENZ & ASSOCIATES, INC.
646 North Michigan Avenue

CRATE AND BARREL HEADQUARTERS, INC. 2002

RALPH JOHNSON
Perkins & Will
725 Landwehr Road, Northbrook, Illinois

In 1987 the Chicago retail firm of Crate and Barrel commissioned a new flagship store in River North. Fitting a 40,000-square-foot facility on an 8,000-square-foot site presented the first challenge to the architects of Solomon Cordwell Buenz. Their solution—four stories of housewares and furniture—required a dazzling space that would encourage shoppers to venture up through the levels. And finally, their building needed to draw people to a neighborhood that, at the time, was not known for retail.

The design is a departure from the traditional retail models on Michigan Avenue. The extensive use of glass and white powder-coated panels resulted in a luminous, modern building, in keeping with the merchandise offered inside. The corner is anchored with a large circular atrium containing the escalators. The transparency and clear circulation routes have overcome the potential drawbacks of multilevel shopping. The store is an attractive, lively, and highly successful retail space.

Crate and Barrel again showed its commitment to classic modern design by commissioning Ralph Johnson of Perkins & Will to design its new headquarters. The facility, completed in 2002, is located on a twenty-four-acre wooded site in Northbrook, a suburb of Chicago. It is composed of two main parts: the offices and the merchandising spaces, where sample products are reviewed. Both are linked by a large glazed lobby. The office spaces are organized like a comb to create courtyards that maximize natural light inside the building and allow wonderful views to the exterior. The spectacular roof, cantilevered from central columns, seems to float above the whole complex.

ABOVE

SOLOMON CORDWELL BUENZ & ASSOCIATES

Elevation of Crate and Barrel Store, 1988. Graphite and colored pencil on white paper on blue paper background.
Gift of Solomon Cordwell Buenz & Associates.

LEFT

SOLOMON CORDWELL BUENZ & ASSOCIATES

Store interior.

RIGHT

PERKINS & WILL

Crate and Barrel Headquarters.

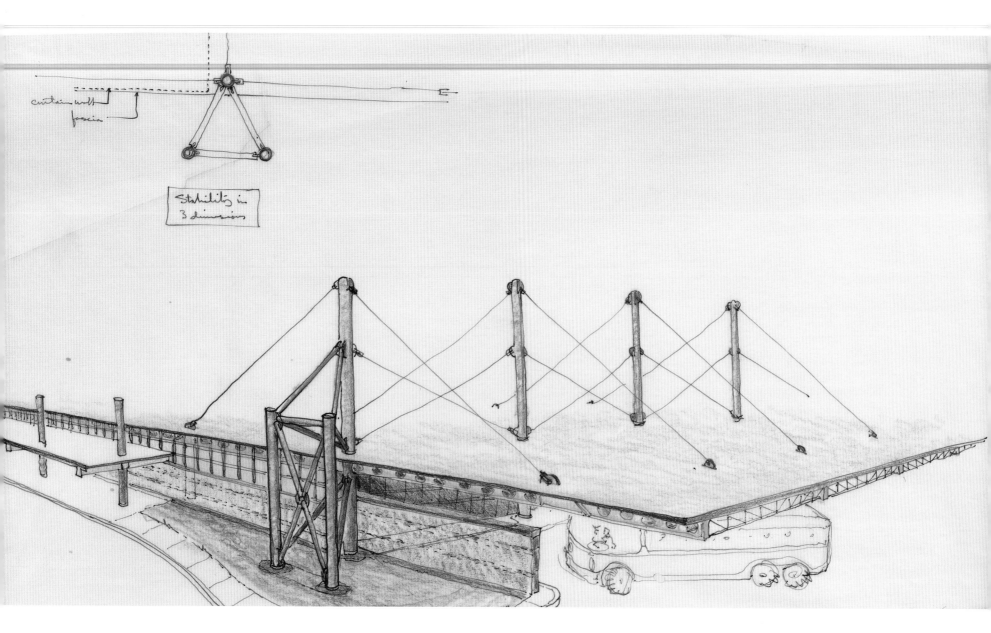

In the sketch, handwritten annotations read: "curtain wall fascia" and "Stability in 3 dimensions".

GREYHOUND/TRAILWAYS BUS TERMINAL
1991

NAGLE HARTRAY & ASSOCIATES

630 West Harrison Street

As part of a nationwide program to revitalize its passenger terminals, Greyhound Lines, Inc., commissioned a prototype facility to replace the thirty-five-year-old terminal in Chicago's Loop. The new building, located just west of the Loop, contains 35,000 square feet of enclosed space devoted to the passenger arrival and departure areas, operations offices, baggage handling, and parcel shipping. The second floor of the building

NAGLE HARTRAY & ASSOCIATES

Sketch of roof suspension system for Greyhound/ Trailways Chicago Bus Terminal, del. Jack Hartray, n.d. Ink, graphite, and colored pencil on yellow tracing paper. Gift of Nagle Hartray & Associates.

houses administrative offices, which overlook the passenger lounge.

The north and south exterior walls have a concrete base and masonry veneer. Horizontal bands of brick emphasize the building's streamlined envelope. The east and west exterior walls are sheathed in corrugated metal siding. Perhaps the most striking element of the terminal is the dynamic roofline. Steel masts rise up to support

large canopy girders. The requirement for two bus canopies with 45-foot spans and unobstructed space below led to the structural solution. The underside of the canopy exposes steel joists and perforated girders to give a delicate appearance. The colors and materials and the structural design itself have given the neighborhood a distinctive landmark that is functional and pleasing to both vehicular and pedestrian traffic.

INTERNATIONAL TERMINAL 1993

RALPH JOHNSON
Perkins & Will
O'Hare International Airport

The International Terminal at O'Hare forms a striking gateway for the airport complex. Sited along the access highway running east-west, the dramatic 800-foot-long arc of the ticketing pavilion establishes a strong image for passengers approaching the airport. This idea, advanced by many generations of architects for air travel, has its roots in the monumental entry arches of train stations of the late nineteenth and early twentieth centuries.

The terminal is also meant to recall an aircraft wing with its smooth, taut exterior and skeletal, delicate interior. The control tower on the runway side acts as a fulcrum, balancing the parts of the overall composition. It was especially challenging to link the terminal and the people mover to the airport's other terminal buildings. Principal designer Ralph Johnson gained more of the site for the International Terminal by placing the train stop inside the building at mid-level. Departing passengers cross over the tracks to arrive at the departure hall.

The International Terminal accommodates foreign airplane departures and all international arrivals at a twenty-one-gate facility. Housed within the three-level structure are all the functions of a bustling airline terminal: the ticketing pavilion, concessions, departure areas, and federal inspection services for incoming passengers, as well as baggage handling and support services.

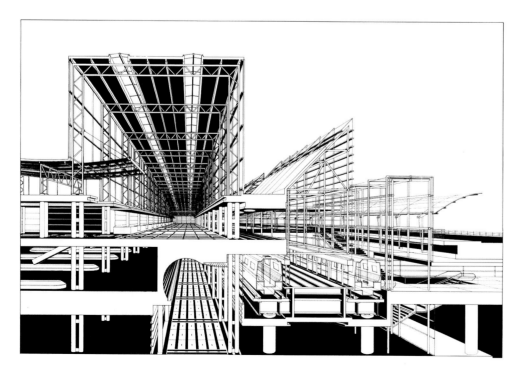

PERKINS & WILL

Interior views and cutaway of the International Terminal, 1989–92/93, del. Ralph Johnson. Ink on mylar and tracing paper. Gifts of Ralph Johnson.

FOLLOWING PAGES

International Terminal at night.

LITTLE VILLAGE ACADEMY 1996

CAROL ROSS BARNEY

Ross Barney + Jankowski Architects
2620 South Lawndale

This public school, located in the heart of Chicago's Hispanic community, opened in 1996 and serves approximately 675 students. The small site required very efficient use of space in order to accommodate the program requirements for classrooms, a library, a cafeteria, and play areas.

The architects, led by Carol Ross Barney, also wanted to create a landmark for the community. This was accomplished by organizing the building around a central staircase that serves as the functional and spiritual heart of the school. As seen from the outside, the three-story volume that encloses the staircase clearly indicates

ABOVE

ROSS BARNEY + JANKOWSKI ARCHITECTS

East elevation of Little Village Academy, 1994. Colored pencil and graphite on yellow tracing paper. Gift of Carol Ross Barney.

RIGHT

Site plan of Little Village Academy, 1994. Colored pencil and graphite on yellow tracing paper. Gift of Carol Ross Barney.

the main entrance to the building. The curved, skylit interior space is highlighted by a large vertical sundial. A sunburst motif is inlaid in the terrazzo floor the lobby and the outdoor plaza. Unique architectural elements contribute to a vibrant building. Visible from the exterior are horizontal sunshades that filter light to the computer room, angled fiberglass walls that create greenhouse space in the science room, and the curved yellow wall of the cafeteria that swells into the playground. The school has received numerous awards for its architecture, appropriate construction, and successful contribution to the community.

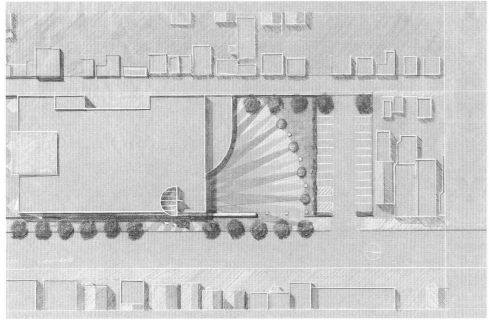

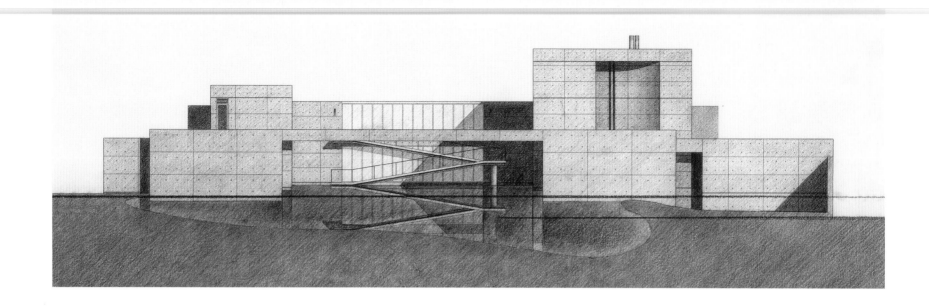

HOUSE IN LINCOLN PARK 1998

TADAO ANDO

Internationally acclaimed Japanese architect Tadao Ando used his signature minimalist architecture and masterfully executed concrete for the single-family home he designed in the Lincoln Park area of Chicago. The house comprises basically three parts: a two-story entry and guest wing at the front, a three-story private wing at the back, and a single-level living/dining area in the middle. The floor-to-ceiling glass panels of the elongated living area allow views to the curving reflecting pool. The 2,000-square-foot pool is an extension of the living area, blurring the division between interior and exterior. Ando has placed concrete walls in the pool to act as screens and to underscore the concept that the pool is an exterior room or extension of the house. Just outside a living room door, a small platform hovers over the water and signals the beginning of the exterior ramp that leads up to the roof terrace. The plain exterior walls of the house shut out the bustle of the street and focus attention on the tranquil space inside. Ando's subdued architecture successfully makes a statement about the relationship between architecture, light, water, and nature.

TADAO ANDO

Elevation of courtyard of House in Lincoln Park. Graphite and colored pencil on paper, ca. 1995. Gift of Tadao Ando.

NEAR RIGHT

TADAO ANDO

View of interior courtyard.

FAR RIGHT

TADAO ANDO

Exterior pool.

MARKOW RESIDENCE 1998

DOUGLAS GAROFALO

Garofalo Architects
Prospect Heights, Illinois

Once a typical suburban split-level in the northwest area of Prospect Heights, this house was altered in the late 1990s to become what the architects call a "suburban intervention." The theoretical basis of the project stems from the belief that suburbia may not be as homogeneous as people are led to believe. The architects, Douglas Garofalo, with Ellen Grimes and Minkyu Whang, saw their work on this project as a series of techniques and effects to modify existing domestic forms and patterns so that new ones could emerge.

The addition to the original house consists basically of three elements: the large double-height central area, or "tube," which cuts through the house; a new volume, cantilevered over the existing foundation and reaching out at the front of the house; and a folding metal roof system that seems to have been created by pulling up and inverting the existing gables. Colors accentuate the play of these three elements.

The interior spaces are laced together with steel and glass stairs, a ramp, and a bridge, all of which wind around the curving central core that contains the bathroom. The materials employed throughout the house include steel, plexiglass, slate, dyed plywood, and translucent fiberglass.

RIGHT

GARAFALO ARCHITECTS

Exploded views of Markow House, 1997–98. Digital presentation by Robert Brobson. Color computer print on paper. Gift of Douglas Garafalo.

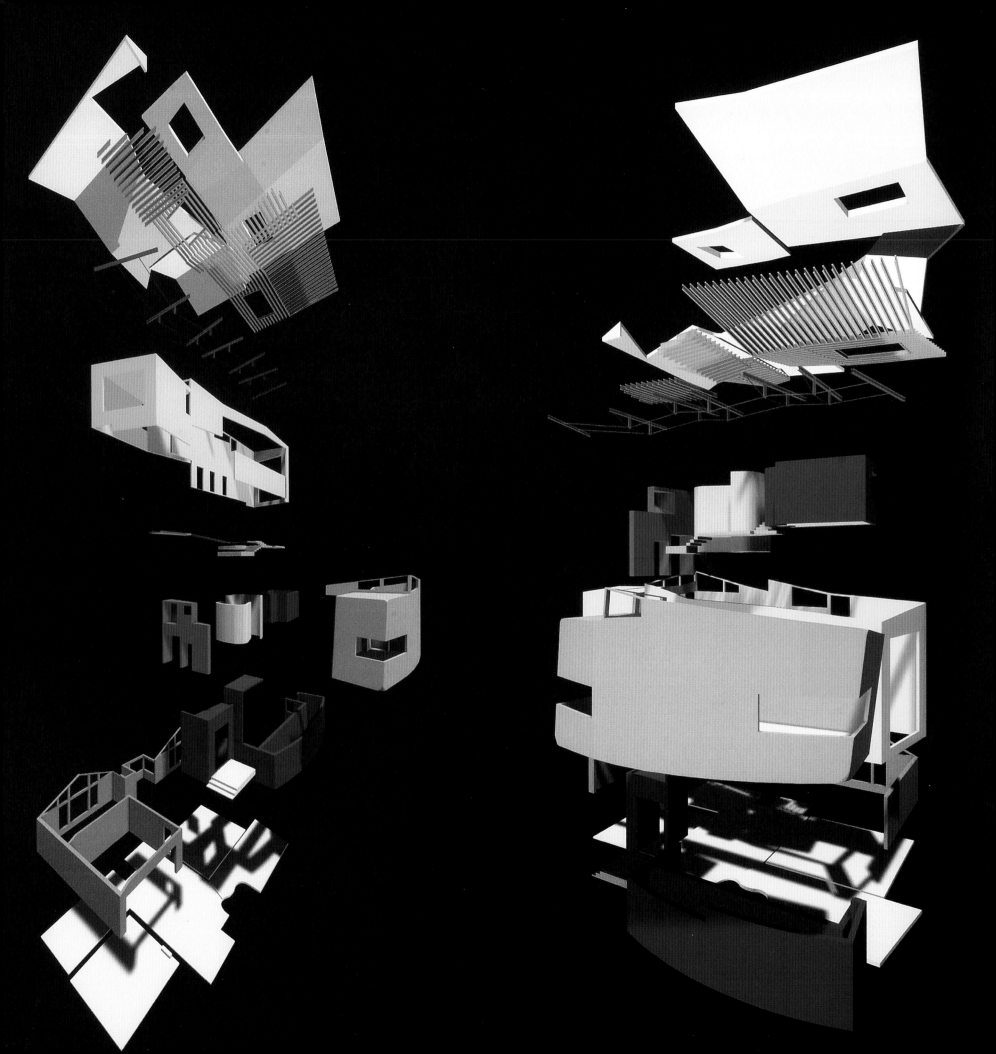

BLUE CROSS/BLUE SHIELD OF ILLINOIS 1998

JAMES GOETTSCH

Lohan Associates
300 East Randolph Street

The sleek blue headquarters of Blue Cross/Blue Shield of Illinois is located just north of the Art Institute of Chicago. Typically, corporations undertaking the construction of a new office building commission one that is larger than their current needs to allow for future growth and expansion. Another conventional means of corporate expansion is through the construction of a second building adjacent to an original. In the case of the new Blue Cross/Blue Shield building, designed by Jim Goettsch, however, the structure of 33 stories was constructed to allow future vertical expansion by the addition of 24 stories on top.

The lobby, with dramatic escalators, is designed not only for the present building population of 4,200, but also for the 7,500 people who will be employed here when the building is fully built-out. The elements of vertical circulation play a particularly important role for the expansion of the building to its ultimate height. They assist in possible future construction and facilitate movement of building materials to the top. The north side of the lobby is an atrium that rises up through the entire building. Currently sixteen elevators serve the building. Space in the atrium was reserved for the addition of sixteen more elevators to serve the added floors.

RIGHT

LOHAN ASSOCIATES

Perspective view of atrium and conference/lounge area on several floors, Blue Cross/Blue Shield Headquarters Building, 1994. Black and white print. Gift of Lohan Associates.

ADLER PLANETARIUM AND
ASTRONOMICAL MUSEUM EXPANSION 1995–99

DIRK LOHAN

Lohan Associates
1300 South Lake Shore Drive

Funded by philanthropist and vice president of Sears Roebuck and Company Max Adler, the first public planetarium in the country was built in Chicago in 1930. The new planetarium and museum exhibited astronomy so successfully that advisors to the Century of Progress Exposition in Chicago in 1933–34 decided that a new Hall of Science was not necessary at the fair. The Adler Planetarium already fit the bill.

The building designed by Ernest Grunsfeld is located on parkland extending into Lake Michigan on axis with the Field Museum. The strong geometric form—

LOHAN ASSOCIATES

West elevation of Adler Planetarium and Astronomy Museum Addition, ca. 1995. Graphite and ink on white vellum-finish tracing paper. Gift of Lohan Associates.

a twelve-sided structure with a protruding central dome—is clad in variegated rainbow granite. The ornamentation of the building includes a carved zodiac sign at each corner and bronze plaques by Alfonso Ianelli. This design won Grunsfeld the American Institute of Architects' Gold Medal of 1931.

A 1975 underground addition, by the firm of C.F. Murphy, increased the square footage of the building, but maintained the exterior appearance of the original. With a more substantial addition required many years later, Lohan Associates (now Lohan Caprile Goettsch) have wrapped the eastern half of the building with a 95,000-square-foot ring of above-ground galleries capped by a wedge-shaped roof. Lohan's design does not attempt to match the existing materials. Rather, his straightforward use of steel and glass for the addition, which crouches down toward the lake, forms an elegant counterpoint to the building of the 1930s.

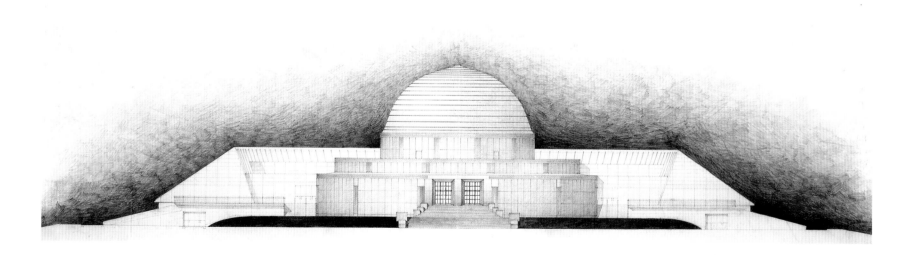

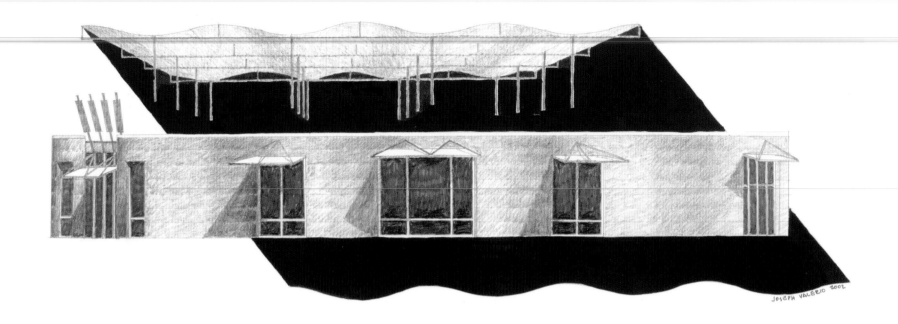

LINCOLN PARK ZOO MAIN STORE AND ROOFTOP CAFÉ 1999

JOE VALERIO

Valerio Dewalt Train

A new two-level building for a store and café is located at the center of the Lincoln Park zoo campus at the transition between the lower, southern portion of the zoo and the higher, northern one. The very first zoo building—an 1889 red brick structure with a hipped roof and walls punctuated by arches—was originally on this site. The nineteenth-century building was completed in a Prairie Style, but was subsequently transformed beyond recognition. Because the building lacked any heritage worth saving, the master plan of 1996 called for replacing it with a new facility.

The architects, led by Joe Valerio, were asked to design not only the new building, but the stairs and sur-

rounding landscaping to link the upper and lower portions of the site. The wide steps and landings form platforms that hug the new building. The curved brick wall, which defines the outer edge of the steps, pays homage to the brick arches of the original building. The main entrance of the new building and the first-floor store are located adjacent to the steps. The building's longest facade, also a curved brick wall, echoes the form initiated with the steps. The second-floor café is topped with a fabric canopy that repeats the wave pattern in elevation rather than plan.

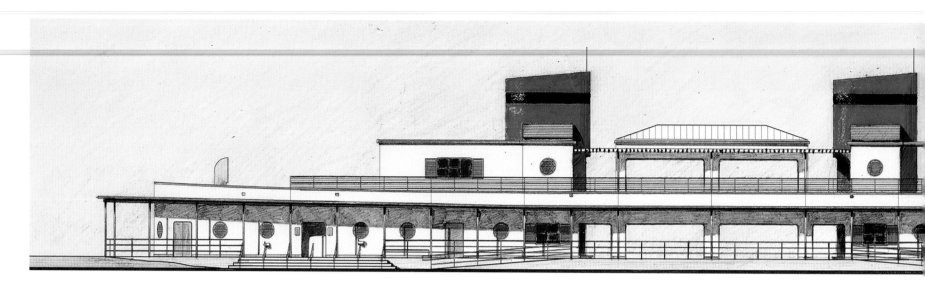

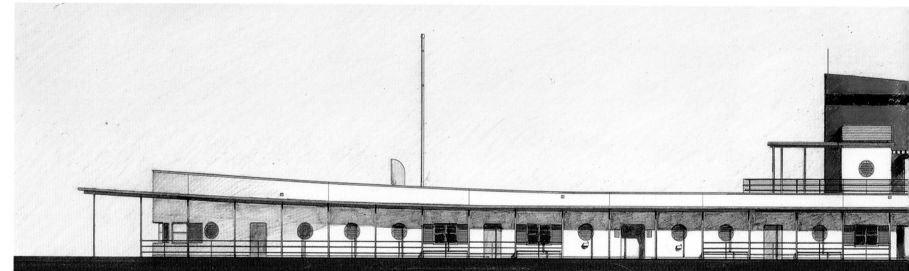

NORTH AVENUE BEACH HOUSE 1999

DAN WHEELER

Wheeler Kearns Architects
GEC Design Group, associated architects
Lake Front, near North Avenue

A much-loved wooden beach house built in 1939 at North Avenue Beach had, by the early 1990s, deteriorated beyond repair. The single-story public structure was a local landmark. The challenge facing the architects of Wheeler Kearns was to respond to public sensitivities and preservation pressure in order to create a new facility that recalled the streamlined and nautical appearance of the original structure.

WHEELER KEARNS ARCHITECTS

Two of four elevations of North Avenue Beach House, 1999. Ink, graphite, and colored pencil on white paper.
Gift of Wheeler Kearns Architects.

The new building, which houses changing rooms, first-aid facilities, and food concessions, was constructed slightly south of the old site. By shifting the new construction off the axis of the nearby streets, views to the lake were opened up. The location of the new building, at a curve in the beachfront, allowed the architects to distance it from the previously congested area where pedestrians, bike, and vehicular traffic all came together. It also meant that the new building could not be lineal, as the old one, but would need to allow vistas on all sides.

The original scheme called for an elliptical building fully clad in louvers. The louvers, when open, would permit access and views to the interior and through the

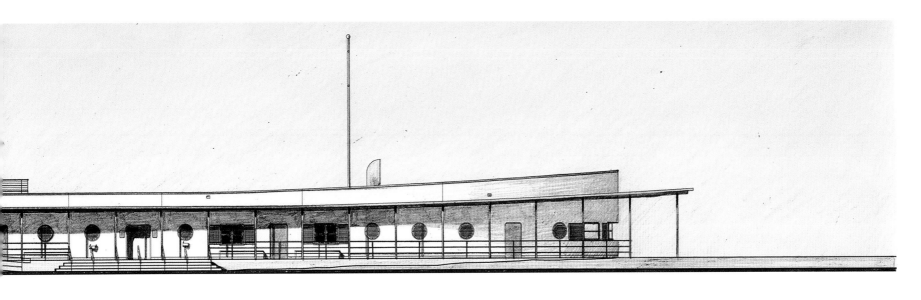

building, or when closed, fully protect the building. The final design accepted by the city was, however, a more literal interpretation of the original North Avenue Beach house. Today's result has a boat-like appearance measuring 20 feet in the center at the widest part and tapering at the ends as the prow of a ship. A thin promenade canopy circling the beach house uses columns equal in diameter and spacing to the original 1939 ones. The two large smokestacks, also recalling the previous structure, are truly functional, housing the resonant open-air metal stairs that lead to the upper deck. The new building proudly fulfills its mission to be a playful structure, a recreation facility, and a civic landmark.

St. Patrick's Roman Catholic Church

Renovation 2000

LAURENCE BOOTH

Booth Hansen Associates
140 S. Desplaines Street

Founded in 1846, St. Patrick's Roman Catholic Church is housed in Chicago's oldest public building. The interior of Old St. Patrick's had been decorated with beautiful Celtic designs in 1915 by Thomas O'Shaughnessy. Numerous subsequent interventions in the twentieth century diluted the purity of the Celtic stenciling on the walls. The stained-glass windows were the only reminders of the Celtic motif. Booth Hansen Associates were commissioned in the 1990s to envision a master plan for revitalizing the church campus as well as to renovate and repair the exterior and to artistically "reunify" the interior of the church itself.

The main floor is subtly reconfigured with a new circular altar at one end and a new baptismal font at the other. The cherry pews of the 876-seat sanctuary are set in a double curve enhancing the sense of gathering together and community (in contrast to traditional stare-straight-ahead pews). The new stenciling takes its inspiration again from Celtic heritage and is in harmony with the stained-glass windows. A new three-arched altar screen that depicts the Creation story echoes the three doorways of the church.

The materials and construction techniques combine traditional craft and modern techniques. The decorative wall stencils were applied as in the past, using paint passed through cut-out screens. The marble inlay pattern for the altar was, however, achieved with computer-assisted technology to guide the cutting tools.

BOOTH HANSEN ASSOCIATES

Interior elevation of nave, detail of stenciling, for interior renovation of St. Patrick's Roman Catholic Church, 2000. Graphite, watercolor, and gold inlay on watercolor paper. Gift of Laurence O. Booth.

HOTEL SOFITEL 2002

JEAN-PAUL VIGUIER

Jean-Paul Viguier, Paris, France
Teng & Associates, associate architects
20 East Chestnut Street

Opened in the summer of 2002 in the city's famed Gold Coast neighborhood, this 412-room Sofitel is one of several hotels built during a recent hotel industry boom in Chicago. To compete with other major chains such as the Hyatt or Hilton, Sofitel sought to use architectural design as one of its distinguishing factors. According to architect Jean-Paul Viguier's design statement, his major concern was to create a composition that "articulates the horizontal elements for public spaces and the vertical elements for private spaces, a structured geometry in a contemporary French classical tradition." To realize this goal, he stacked 27 stories of guestrooms on top of a five-story base of public spaces and reception areas. The tower, a triangular wedge, tilts outward over the sidewalk and narrows as it rises.

The prism-shaped hotel, skillfully utilizing its corner position, creates a public plaza and outdoor café at the main entrance on Chestnut Street. The hotel has two prominent facades with exposures facing east and southwest; together they allow natural light to reach well into the interior. Defined by its alternating layers of glass and polished stone, the tower projects smoothly out from the site, creating an "emblematic figure" unlike other block-like structures in Chicago's architectural grid.

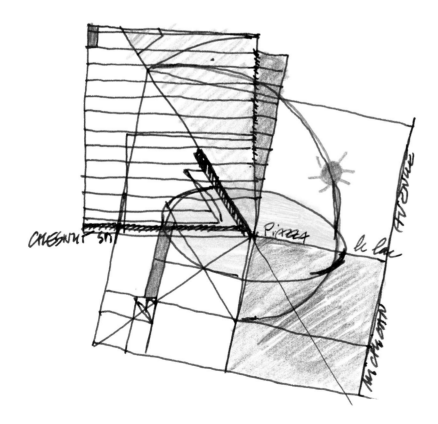

JEAN-PAUL VIGUIER

Preliminary design study for site plan of Hotel Sofitel, 2002. Ink and crayon on white paper. Gift of Jean-Paul Viguier.

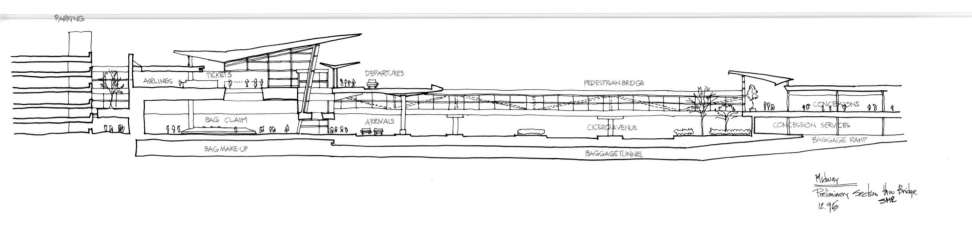

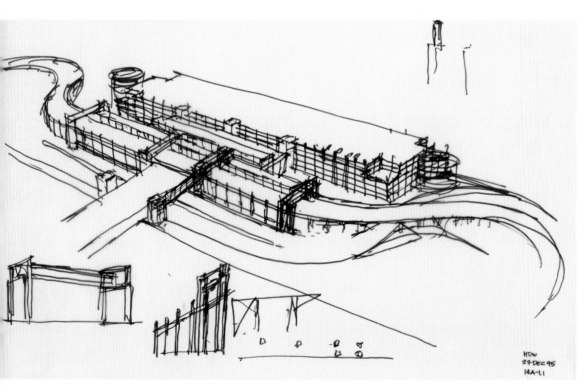

NEW TERMINAL AT MIDWAY AIRPORT
2004

STEVEN REISS

HNTB Architecture

HNTB ARCHITECTURE

Preliminary sketch through
bridge (top) and aerial design
study (bottom) for Midway
Airport Addition, 1995–97.
Pen on white tracing paper
(preliminary sketch); marker
on yellow tracing paper (aerial
study). Gift of Steven M. Reiss,
HNTB Architecture.

Chicago's Municipal Airport was founded 1927 in what
was then a relatively unpopulated, industrial area at the
edge of the city near 57th Street and Cicero Avenue.
Renamed Midway Airport in 1949 after the aerial battle
that turned the tide of the Pacific conflict in World War
II (June 4–7, 1942), Midway became the world's busiest
airport, handling more than 10 million passengers in
1959. Even though Chicago's famous O'Hare
International Airport (see pp. 118, 164, and 182) far sur-
passed Midway as the world's busiest, Chicago's older,
in-town airport witnessed renewed traffic after the 1978
deregulation of the airlines. Today, Midway hosts more
than 15 million travelers a year. That increased traffic
warranted a new terminal to replace the aging, smaller
1947 building. Steven Reiss of HNTB designed the new
complex of 900,000 square feet, moving the check-in
and arrival areas to the east of Cicero to gain valuable
space, and connecting the gates west of Cicero with a
dramatic concourse that acts like a bridge to span the
avenue. The architect utilized a palette of materials that
relate to local building traditions, particularly the light
bricks used in bungalows throughout Chicago's neighborhoods, as well as a clock tower to punctuate the complex as if it were a neighborhood monument.

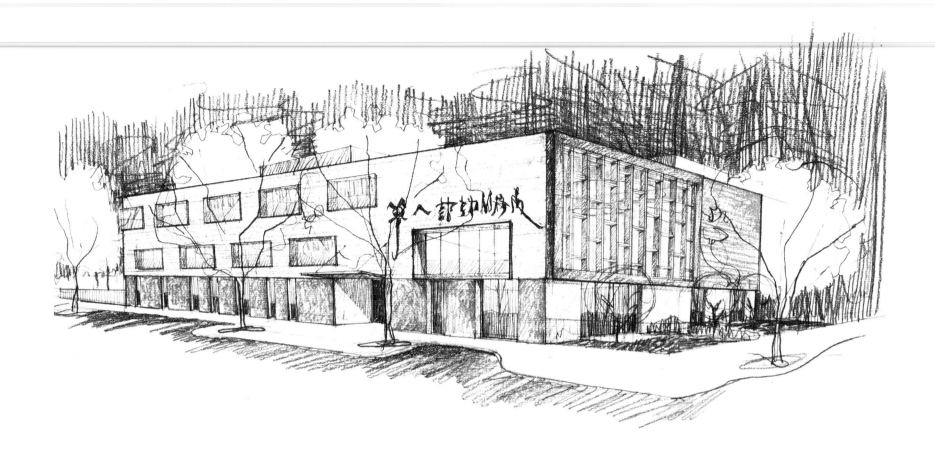

CHINESE AMERICAN SERVICE CENTER 2003

JEANNE GANG

Studio Gang/O'Donnell
2141 South Tan Court

This 38,000-square-foot building designed to serve multiple community functions began with a competition in 1999. Of the six teams that made it to the final round, the firm of Studio Gang/O'Donnell (now Studio Gang Architects)was selected to develop the building located in Chicago's Chinatown area.

The new three-story facility for the Chinese American Service League brings activities currently housed in four different locations under one roof. The program includes space for child and adult daycare, counseling and conference rooms, after-school classrooms, a chef's training kitchen, and administrative offices. The largest single area is a double height multipurpose room called the Community Hall. Although preliminary designs

STUDIO GANG/O'DONNELL

Perspective rendering of Chinese American Service Center, 2001. Graphite and colored pencil on white paper, shown with computer-generated views, right.
Gift of Jeanne Gang.

placed this on the first floor, the decision was made to move it to the second. This move meant that many spaces that required easy access, such as daycare facilities, could be accommodated at street level and that the two-story Community Hall would become a more visible and symbolic part of the building when seen from the street. This hall faces southwest and is bordered by an exterior balcony. The balcony and exterior steel lattice sunscreen protect the community room from direct solar exposure, reducing energy use. The rest of the building incorporates taut, diamond-shaped metal cladding like a dragon's skin. Two different finishes of titanium alternate across the building's surface giving depth to its appearance.

CHICAGO IN THE NEW MILLENNIUM

MARTHA THORNE

Chicago has a special place within the history of American cities, nowhere more so than in architecture. It quickly grew from a frontier settlement to a bustling urban center; first incorporated as a city in 1837, by 1890 it had more than a million residents. The tragic fire of 1871 reduced much of the city's stock to ashes. But following that catastrophe came a rebirth marked by an unprecedented building effort that, combined with industrial-era advances, spurred innovation. Architects moved away from wood to fireproofed iron and steel construction. Those advances made tall structures buildable, and the new safety elevator made them usable. Chicago's skyline was radically altered after 1880. Where five-story buildings were once the norm, new "towers" of ten to twenty stories sprang up, including the ten-story Montauk Block (1882) by Burnham & Root, sometimes called Chicago's first skyscraper; the Home Insurance Building of 1884-85 by William LeBaron Jenney, also ten stories, but with metal framing; and slightly later in the 1890s, many more examples, such as the Reliance and Fisher buildings by Burnham & Root, or the Auditorium and Chicago Stock Exchange Building by Adler & Sullivan.

Chicago defeated New York in the bid to host the 1893 World's Colombian Exposition. The "White City" was constructed by leading stylemakers of Chicago and their East Coast colleagues under the direction of Daniel Burnham. It was a Beaux Arts fantasyland a few miles south of the Loop, in what was previously an area of sand and swamp, skillfully landscaped by Frederick Law Olmsted. For many, this spectacular architectural show further enhanced Chicago's reputation. The effect was much longer lasting than the fair itself. New cultural and educational buildings were built in the classical style due to the impetus of the exposition.

Burnham along with Edward H. Bennett again catalyzed interest in the city's built environment and its future through the creation of *The Plan of Chicago*, published in 1909 and supported by Commercial Club. This visionary master plan, reflected in beautifully illustrated drawings, addressed issues including transportation, urban spaces, the lakefront, and even building heights. With hundreds of meetings held during the preparation of the Plan and the promotion of it in the years following its publication, the Plan was widely known within and outside of Chicago. Once again, the city showed its capacity for leading the way in architecture and planning.

In much of the twentieth century, Chicago continued to use architecture to assert itself. The back-and-forth battle with New York to construct the tallest building in the world began in the late 1800s and raged throughout the twentieth century. Chicago had thrown down the gauntlet in the nineteenth century with the first tall buildings, but in 1913 New York City forged ahead in the race with the 792-foot-high Woolworth Building. This was followed by the Chrysler Building in 1929 and then the Empire State Building in 1931, which remained the world's tallest building until 1972. Then, the World Trade Center in New York dominated for a short period until, in 1974, the Sears Tower was built in Chicago. To date, this building still has the highest occupied floor and greatest height to the roof in the world.

The history of twentieth-century American architecture would not be complete without the inclusion of two

RIGHT

PERKINS & WILL

Computer-rendered perspective of Skybridge Condominium Building, 2002.

Chicago giants: Frank Lloyd Wright and Ludwig Mies van der Rohe. Both influenced architecture in Chicago as well as internationally.

Frank Lloyd Wright is undoubtedly America's most famous architect, credited with originating the Prairie Style. His pioneering work in architecture, especially residential design, but also in urban planning and in building technology, continues to be the subject of study and admiration today.

Mies, who arrived in Chicago in 1938 to head Armour Institute (now Illinois Institute of Technology), had a profound effect on the city through his buildings as well as his teachings. Not only did he revamp the curriculum at IIT and design its new campus buildings, but his numerous disciples and followers went on to apply the International Style to corporate and government buildings in Chicago and across the U.S. for decades to come.

In the 1970s and early 1980s, in response to the ideas put forth by Mies and his disciples and perhaps to break the domination that big firms had on architecture, the group known as the Chicago Seven was formed. In a climate of economic recession and Chicago's waning contemporary architectural reputation, the members of the group energized debate and pushed their ideas on architecture to the forefront through exhibitions, writings, discussions, and competitions. The original group of seven (Tom Beeby, Larry Booth, Stuart Cohen, James I. Freed, James Nagle, Stanley Tigerman, and Ben Weese) soon expanded to also include Helmut Jahn, Cynthia Weese, Gerald Horn, and Ken Schroeder. Perhaps the diversity of their approaches to architecture precluded a long-term, stable group structure. Nonetheless, the

Chicago Seven questioned the status quo, enlivened debate, and laid the foundation for the establishment of the Chicago Architecture Club, a loose and vibrant forum for debate and discussion by architects and colleagues that still exists today.

A significant part of Chicago's reputation has been based on its position as a leading force in American building trends. Therefore, its architecture is constantly analyzed and reviewed, and its leadership role scrutinized. Attempts to define Chicago's current position and contributions to contemporary architecture, as well as to advance theories about its future direction are popular subjects for discussions, public and private alike. Different aspects of the debate on the "state of Chicago's architecture" are reflected in newspapers, symposia, exhibitions, and informal gatherings. Debate has heated up in the recent past. If commentaries by some critics are true, then since the 1990s Chicago has relinquished its leadership in architectural innovation and quality. The recent round of discussion was kicked off and concisely articulated by Blair Kamin in a January 1996 article in the *Chicago Tribune*. He declared, "After reigning for more than a century as the unofficial capital of American architecture, Chicago's pre-eminence has vanished—its crown knocked off, its nerve lost, its capacity for greatness diminished" ("Structural Damage," *Chicago Tribune*, Jan. 21, 1996). When it comes to the last decade of construction in the city, Kamin's motto is "too much building, too little quality."

It is often said that Chicago's architectural conservatism can be attributable to clients' attitudes and the national business climate. Those who make loans for buildings—the heads of banks or insurance companies—often take a well-worn path, shying away from anything new or different. The East Coast and West Coast, with strong fashion and film industries, seem to take more risks. This idea was further discussed in another extensive article that appeared in the *Chicago Reader* in January 2003. Author Lynn Becker echoed such sentiments, stating, "Chicago—a city at the center of world architecture for over a century—could be closing out a building boom that won't produce a single structure of international significance." She noted that Chicago's aesthetic collapse is not part of an overall national trend, but is place-specific. Much of the blame, in Becker's opinion, rests with private development.

Amid these gloomy and rather vocal opinions, it is worth reevaluating Chicago's current architectural scene. And, there are solid reasons for optimism in the general situation, in exemplary firms and projects, and in the work of organizations and institutions devoted to the city's built environment.

The practice of architecture has always been important in Chicago. There is no doubt that cities with a critical mass of professionals, schools of architecture, and related organizations have a better chance at creating a vital and interesting forum for architecture. Chicago is one of these. The schools and departments of architecture at the University of Illinois at Chicago, Illinois Institute of Technology, and School of the Art Institute have been gaining ground recently with talented professors and administrators and a larger and more competitive pool of applicants, especially at the graduate level. The students of these institutions will be the architects and policymakers of the future.

There are more than 2,500 members of the American Institute of Architects in the four counties of the Chicago chapter. Membership in the AIA is not obligatory for architects, and it is estimated that the total number of architects in the Chicago area is closer to 4,000. The AIA 2003 directory lists 393 firms in the area employing 3,142 licensed architects and graduates of architecture schools. Firm sizes range from single-person offices to McClier with 425 employees (105 of whom are architects). Other large firms include Teng Associates with 375 employees (83 architects), OWPP with 335 employees (152 architects, 71 engineers, and 15 registered landscape architects or interior designers), and A. Epstein & Sons with 270 employees (70 architects). Also in the ten largest: Perkins & Will with 239 employees (97 architects); Skidmore, Owings & Merrill, once the most powerful firm in the city, today has 239 employees (92 architects and 76 engineers); and DeStafano Keating Partners with 144 employees (89 architects). OWPP led all firms in volume of Chicago-area construction in 2002 at $700 million each (*Crain's Chicago Business*, Feb. 3, 2003, p. 17).

The majority of architecture firms were established in the 1980s and 1990s. However, about 10 percent have been in existence only since 2000, which seems to indicate both a general stability in the field and room for new and emerging firms.

When compared with the past ten years, the situation today seems favorable. The AIA membership figures have risen, from 1,835 members in 1994, to 2,192 members in 1998, to the current figure of 2,638 members. In 1994 there were 312 firms in Chicago and today there are 393, a 26 percent increase. Compensation at architectural firms has continued to steadily increase in the past years despite the slowdown in the economy. The average compensation for architects at firms in the city of Chicago is ahead of the national average except at the junior level.

Architectural building activity in Chicago is many times spurred by public investment or private developers. While some unsuccessful buildings were constructed in the recent past, perhaps due to developers' needs for expediency or economic constraints, or a general conservative attitude on the part of the city's administration, some exceptions are worth noting. One is the residential high-rise Skybridge, designed by Ralph Johnson of Perkins & Will. The tower, located just west of the Loop along the expressway, takes full advantage of its setting while meeting the developer's requirements. The building rises over 420 feet using an interesting play of solids and transparent volumes. It is almost like two thin towers linked by a series of transparent bridges. The clear differentiation of the functional parts of the building and its oversized canopy grant it a powerful, sculptural quality.

Lucien LaGrange's striking new residential tower at 500 West Erie is another unconventional and quality addition to Chicago's skyline. The modern building, a parallelogram of glass and steel, uses a structural system of exterior lateral bracing that further enhances its presence on the tight urban site. UBS Tower at 1 North Wacker, designed by James Goettsch of Lohan Caprile Goettsch, is a recent positive contribution to Chicago's downtown. Even if the upper part of the office tower is rather standard, the building makes a successful connection to the street with its cable and glass lobby-wall. Lining the street are trees set in giant semi-circular berms, providing attractive landscaping and a positive response to security concerns. And finally, Jean-Paul Viguier designed the Sofitel (see p. 210) as a private endeavor and made an enormous leap forward in the traditional Chicago high-rise hotel.

An interesting rebuttal to examples of unimaginative architecture in Chicago can be seen in several institutional

projects. Currently, some of the most daring new buildings are being undertaken at academic institutions. In 1998 Illinois Institute of Technology hired Rem Koolhaas of the Office of Metropolitan Architecture in Rotterdam to design its new McCormick Tribune Campus Center after an invited competition of five of the most outstanding designers of the day. (In addition to Koolhaas, the architects were Zaha Hadid, Helmut Jahn and Werner Sobek, Peter Eisenman, and Kazuo Seijima.) The selected design creates a unique new focal point for the university while it seeks to link the east and west parts of the campus. A low building situated under the elevated public transit line will house food courts, student organization offices, retail shops, a recreational facility, and a space for

OFFICE FOR METROPOLITAN ARCHITECTURE (OMA)

McCormick Tribune Campus Center, Illinois Institute of Technology, 2003.

campus events. At one corner of the new project an existing original building by Mies is integrated into the new construction. The most striking visual element of the campus center is the giant 560-foot steel tube encasing the track of the Green Line train, directly above the main structure. The tube buffers the noise of the passing train.

Nearby at 33rd and State Streets, just south of the campus center, Helmut Jahn was hired to design a new residence facility serving about 375 IIT students. The dorm is composed of three separate five-story buildings, joined by exterior glass walls screening the El line at the back. The curved facades aligned along State Street form a link between the Mies campus of isolated buildings and the landscape of traditional Chicago neighborhoods. The glass-and-aluminum-clad buildings are certainly modern, yet the courtyards between the buildings and the main facades create a pedestrian-friendly environment.

The University of Chicago, founded in 1890, has recently embarked on a major building campaign for its Hyde Park campus. As a significant part of the plan for new structures needed by the university, architects of international reputation have been commissioned to undertake the designs—a program that will break away from the dominant "collegiate Gothic" style of many the university's original buildings. Beginning with a modest parking structure with some offices by New Haven–based Cesar Pelli, which was completed complete in 2000, the process of hiring non-Chicagoans has expanded.

Cesar Pelli is also the designer of the recently completed Ratner Athletic Center. This 145,000-square-foot building, at 55th Street and Ellis Avenue, houses an Olympic-sized swimming pool, practice gymnasiums, a fitness center, dance classrooms, locker rooms, and administrative facilities. Its wave-like roof supported by tension cables attached to five major and fifteen minor masts is creating a new landmark.

The Palevsky Resdiences by the Mexico-based firm of Legorreta & Legorreta Architects opened in 2001. The three interconnected buildings line the 56th Streets from Ellis to University Avenues. On the interior of the block, plazas and courtyards are formed. The bright colors—

MURPHY/JAHN ARCHITECTS

State Street elevation, State Street Village (student residences), Illinois Institute of Technology, 2003.

purple, yellow, and pink—of the entrance pavilions, common areas, and courtyards and the orange brick of the rest of the residence building contrast sharply with the context of the subdued palette of the university.

The University of Chicago's Graduate School of Business by Rafael Viñoly is projected to be completed in 2004. Viñoly's New York–based office was selected out of six firms in the running for this building on a sensitive site next to Frank Lloyd Wright's Frederick C. Robie House. The new facility, estimated to cost $125 million, will house classes, offices, study rooms, lounges, and food services in a 415,000-square-foot facility. The building with seven floors above ground and two below is organized around a winter garden atrium that is 83 feet tall.

In downtown Chicago, Sheila Kennedy with the firm of Kennedy & Violich (KVA) of Boston was slated to transform the North American Building at the corner of State Street and Monroe Street into a center for technology and design for the School of the Art Institute of Chicago. KVA is known for its multidisciplinary approach to design and visionary use of technology and materials. Although economic considerations have effectively ended the prospects for this project, her innovative design would have been an exciting addition to Chicago's Loop.

Spertus Institute of Jewish Studies has commissioned the Chicago firm of Krueck & Sexton to design the needed expansion of its facilities on Michigan Avenue.

The new building, which is expected to open in 2006, will be located next to the ninety-two-year-old renovated office building that currently houses the Institute. The new facility will respond to the need for enhanced space for the museum, college, and library and will provide classrooms, gallery space, a theater, a restaurant, and other amenities. Architect Ron Krueck is charged with creating a building that will be innovative and contemporary yet complementary to the neighboring historic architecture.

Millennium Park has recuperated a major tract of land just north of the Art Institute for public open space. With the city's initiative and the generosity of private sponsors, the park will have a series of unique features. The overall project for the park, with a master plan by Skidmore, Owings & Merrill, includes an open-air pavil-

ion, a skating rink, peristyle, fountain, garden, music and dance theater, and underground parking. Frank Gehry is constructing the band shell, which will be the most striking element of the new park. The stage is framed by giant stainless steel curls and faces a Great Lawn that is 600 by 300 feet. Seating will be provided on the Great Lawn and a sound system will be suspended from a trellis that will span the lawn's width. The Music and Dance Theater, by the firm of Hammond Beeby Rupert Ainge provides a state-of-the-art facility with 1,500-seat theater for a consortium of twelve of Chicago's music and theater companies. The construction at the north end of the park is mostly underground, but the thin glass entrance pavilion forms a lantern indicating the presence of the theater as well as an appropriate counterpoint to the prominent forms of the Gehry bandshell.

Right across the street from Millennium Park, the Art Institute of Chicago currently plans another addition. Designed by Renzo Piano, the new wing, approximately 220,000 square feet, will be located on the northeast quadrant of the Art Institute's grounds, with a striking new entrance on Monroe Street. The facility will provide much needed space for modern and contemporary art, architecture, and education, among other new areas. The signature element of the glass, steel, and limestone building promises to be its roof of curved panels that will form a protective sunscreen that appears to float above the structure.

Perhaps the most hope for Chicago's future built environment can be found in emerging firms and projects outside the Loop. It is worth keeping an eye on several of them. The office of Garofalo Architects, led by Doug Garofalo, seeks to be a forward-looking practice; their design philosophy states, "Both the products and practice of architectural design can participate in the new developments that are redefining our culture and our environment." Garofalo's firm breaks down both geographic boundaries and those that limit the definition of professional disciplines. In all of Garofalo's projects, there is an attempt to pair technological advances with craftsmanship. Needless to say, the firm uses the computer as a design tool, to enhance communication, and in the construction process. Looking toward the future, the Hyde

RIGHT

KENNEDY VIOLICH ARCHITECTS

Design Initiative Center, School of the Art Institute of Chicago, 2003.

BELOW

RENZO PIANO BUILDING WORKSHOP

Monroe Street elevation, The Art Institute of Chicago Addition, 2002.

GAROFALO ARCHITECTS

Computer-rendered section of
the Hyde Park Arts Center,
2002.

STUDIO GANG/O'DONNELL

Bengt Sjostrom/Starlight
Theater, Rock Valley
Community College,
Rockford, Illinois, 2003,
designed by Jeanne Gang.

Park Art Center promises to be a noteworthy project. The not-for-profit organization, which provides the area with outstanding exhibitions and educational programs, will relocate to an existing two-story masonry structure, formerly used by the University of Chicago Press. Although the building is rather mundane, Garofalo Architects will energize it and the adjacent street by adding glass and steel and a support for experimental electronic installations to the facade. It will allow for many alternative forms of digital projections and electronic art. The project will also perforate the building to bring natural light to the interior and will include a rooftop prairie, visible from the neighboring residential towers.

Studio Gang, a small firm headed by architect Jeanne Gang, is one of Chicago's offices that combines research and practice. A professor at Illinois Institute of

Technology, Gang designs projects that often look to new materials or new uses for traditional materials to create more innovative approaches to building. Outside of Chicago in Rockford, Illinois, she has recently completed the Starlight Theater for Rock Valley College. The amphitheater has a movable roof that can be opened for summer performances or closed for protection against the weather. At the roof's center, six movable triangles form a hexagon that opens in a way similar to petals of a flower.

Brininstool & Lynch is a small but solid firm that began in 1989 with commissions for single-family residences, but they have since expanded to take on larger projects. The Racine Art Museum, opened in May 2003, shows the agility of the firm. Starting with an old building, composed of two parts and multiple structural systems, the architects created a museum of luminous, flowing spaces. They achieved their signature vertical richness by varying ceiling heights and creating multiple views through spaces. The architects have enhanced both the museum's collection and the city. They clad the building in limestone and plastic panels that unify the exterior and permit it to glow at night when the panels are illuminated. In Chicago, the firm has undertaken several residential buildings including one at 1440 South Michigan Avenue, and a second nearby at 1845 South Michigan, just south of Chicago's Loop.

Wilkinson Blender Architecture, Inc., is a neighborhood firm in Chicago's Roscoe Village. One project that represents its creative thinking is Fellger Park. Although the park was originally planned by the city, with the help of neighborhood associations the firm was able to redirect its design. Wilkinson Blender's solution was to design the corner park as a useful open space for all generations. They developed a natural landscape buffer between the street and the park. Multiple "activity maps" were developed relating to each potential activity and were then layered on top of one another to guide the final design. This first modest example points toward exciting future projects from the firm.

The Stateway Gardens area of Chicago, defined by 1950s public housing projects by Holabird Root & Burgee, will undergo a massive transformation with the potential to introduce a development project of the highest quality design. Located three miles south of the Loop from 35th to 39th Streets, eight disastrous high-rises will be torn down and replaced by a new mixed-income community being developed by a private company, Stateway Associates. The construction of 1,316 units, equally distributed between market-rate units for sale, affordable units for sale and rent, and public housing, will be undertaken in three phases. The first units at the northern part of the site will be designed by Kathryn Quinn Architects, Urbanworks, Landon Bone Baker, and William Worn Architects. The second phase of the proposal will include Brook Architects and Patrick Fitzgerald Architects. All of these firms are small but recognized for their quality work. This complex project could make a substantial contribution to the neighborhood as well as to the way development is perceived in the city.

Many other young firms around the city seize the smallest project and try to create sensitive and quality buildings. Ones to watch include 3-D Design with partners Darrell Crosby and Melinda Palmore; John Ronan; and Martin Felson & Sara Dunn, among others.

In its own way, the Department of Architecture at the Art Institute is seeking to reflect the changing face of architectural practice and respond to new and emerging tools and techniques. The department's mission includes collecting, preserving, and making available materials that will record and reflect the city's architectural activity and heritage. While one aspect of collection development involves decisions about which buildings and projects to represent in the collection, there is another facet, perhaps even larger, about choosing which kinds of information to collect in the future.

Architects are moving away from the traditional tools of the trade—pencil and paper—in favor of the computer, relying on it more and more as an integral part of professional practice. This creates a significant challenge in determining the nature of materials to be collected in the future. It is no longer possible to simply review paper documents for an understanding of the design process and then select the most appropriate examples for inclusion in a museum's collection. A multitude of questions arises ranging from a reevaluation of the process of design and the computer's effect upon this to technical issues about how to conserve digital media in order to guarantee its longevity and utility. Curatorial departments of architecture and archives must redefine their collection parameters and capabilities to accommodate the realities of electronic media.

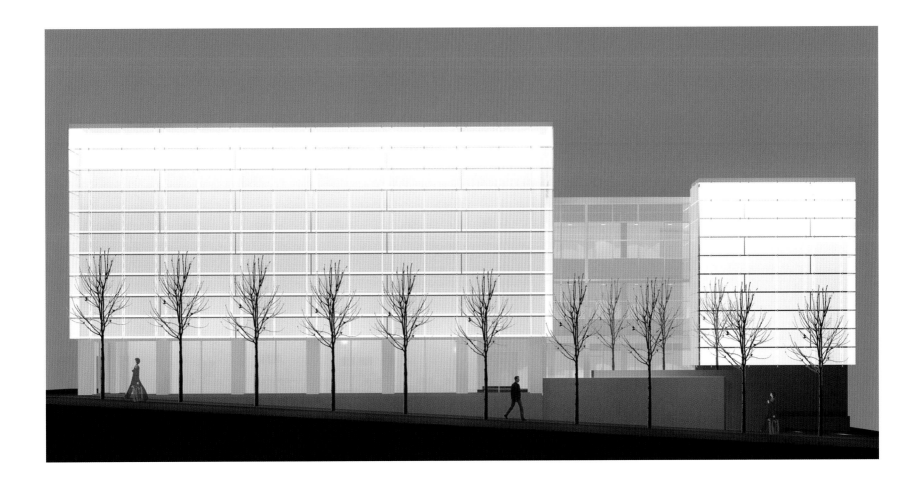

BRININSTOOL + LYNCH, LTD.

Elevation of the Racine Art
Museum, Racine, Wisconsin,
2003.

The Department of Architecture of the Art Institute of
Chicago has begun an eighteen-month study designed to
make an original contribution to the understanding of
procedures for collecting, archiving, and exhibiting digital
design data produced by architects and industrial designers. The goal is to facilitate the acquisition and exhibition
of electronically created architectural designs and to build
a technical capacity that will ensure that such material will
be accessible to scholars and the public. In so doing, we
hope that the Art Institute will be the first institution in
the world to establish standards for collecting and exhibiting digital models for architecture. Additionally, this initiative will pave the way for other museum collections to
replicate or adapt this model as they grapple with the
inevitable impact of new techniques and technology.

Debate about the state of Chicago architecture will no
doubt continue. According to some, it should be recognized for its commercialism and conservatism. Others
maintain that its strong points are innovation and exper-
imentation. In any case, it seems clear that the city has a
dynamic professional community of architects with
numerous excellent firms who can contribute to the
city's architectural future. Work by several of them is
reflected in this publication. Many of the most innovative Chicago buildings today are small in scale and
located outside the downtown area. They are initiated by
enlightened clients who allow for a degree of experi-
mentation and risk in the short term in order to guarantee a long-lasting contribution to the built environment.
Finally, the Art Institute's Department of Architecture is
also responding to the challenges of the future by recog-
nizing the changes taking place within the practice of
architecture and seeking to be innovative in own practice
of collecting. Chicago will always be a city of contrasts
and often-conflicting ideas, but its rich architectural heritage and the current energy and vitality it brings
together mean that its architecture will always be a fun-
damental component. The future of its built environment promises to be even more diverse and exciting. A
city second to none.

WILKINSON BLENDER ARCHITECTURE, INC.

Computer-rendered perspective of Fellger Park, 2002.

APPENDICES
LIST OF SELECTED EXHIBITIONS

Installation design architects, when applicable, listed in parentheses.

LEFT

AEROSPACE DESIGN

Installation, 2003.
Designed by Jeanne Gang.

1981

P.B. Wight: Architect, Contractor, and Critic, 1838–1925

1982

Edward H. Bennett: Architect and City Planner, 1874–1954

Chicago Architects Design: A Century of Architectural Drawings from The Art Institute of Chicago

1983

New Chicago Architecture: Beyond the International Style

1984

Chicago and New York: More Than a Century of Architectural Interactions

Architecture in Context: The Avant-Garde in Chicago's Suburbs—Paul Schweikher and William Ferguson Deknatel

1985

Architecture in Context: The Postwar American Dream

1986

The Unknown Mies van der Rohe and His Disciples of Modernism

1987

Fragments of Chicago's Past (permanent installation by John Vinci)

Architecture in Context: Paul Rudolph—Four Recent Projects in Southeast Asia

1988

The Modern Movement

Chicago Architecture, 1872–1922: Birth of a Metropolis (installation designed by Stanley Tigerman)

1989

Louis Kahn in the Midwest

French Avant-Garde Architecture 1989

Stanley Tigerman: Recent Projects

1990

Emilio Ambasz

1991

Austrian Architecture and Design: Beyond Tradition in the 1990s

1992

Building a New Spain: Contemporary Spanish Architecture

1993

Moscow Avant-Garde Architecture: 1955–1991 (installation designed by Eugene Asse)

Chicago Architecture and Design, 1923–1993: Reconfiguration of an American Metropolis (installation coordinated by Stanley Tigerman with theme spaces designed by Darcy Bonner, Howard Decker, Ronald Krueck, Kathryn Quinn, Christopher Rudolph, Daniel Wheeler, Steven Wierzbowski, Maria Whiteman)

1994

Daniel Libeskind and the Jewish Museum in Berlin (installation designed by Daniel Libeskind)

Renzo Piano Building Workshop—Selected Projects (installation designed by Renzo Piano)

Karl Friedrich Schinkel, 1781–1841: The Drama of Architecture (installation designed by Stanley Tigerman)

1995

Louis Henry Sullivan: From Paris to Chicago

The Architecture of Bruce Goff, 1904–1982: Design for the Continuous Present (installation designed by Bart Prince)

The Prairie School: Selections from the Collections

1996

Contemporary British Architects (installation designed by Nicholas Grimshaw)

D.H. Burnham and Mid-American Classicism

Building for Air Travel: Architecture and Design for Commercial Aviation (installation designed by Helmut Jahn)

1997

Drawn from the Source: The Travel Sketches of Louis I. Kahn (installation designed by Margaret McCurry)

The Grand Tour: Travel Sketches from the Permanent Collection (installation designed by Margaret McCurry)

The Modern Midwestern Landscape: Franz Lipp and Gertrude Kuh (installation designed by Margaret McCurry)

1998

Japan 2000: Architecture and Design for the Japanese Public (installation designed by Hiroshi Ariyama of Hirano Design)

Kisho Kurokawa (installation designed by Kisho Kurokawa)

1999

The Plan of Chicago

The Pritzker Architecture Prize: 1979–1999 (installation designed by Carlos Jimenez)

2000

Bilbao: The Transformation of a City (installation designed by Xavier Vendrell)

Skyscrapers: The New Millennium (installation designed by Ralph Johnson of Perkins & Will)

2001

2001: Building for Space Travel (installation designed by Douglas Garofalo)

Modern Trains and Splendid Stations (installation designed by David Childs and Marilyn Taylor of Skidmore, Owings & Merrill)

2002

Helmut Jacoby: Master of Architectural Drawing

David Adler, Architect: The Elements of Style (installation designed by Laurence Booth)

2003

Aerospace Design (installation designed by Jeanne Gang, p. 234)

Recent Acquisitions (installation designed by Brad Lynch of Bininstool & Lynch)

ACKNOWLEDGMENTS

A book such as this is the result of decades of collecting both historic artifacts and information. Countless people have, thus, contributed to the body of knowledge presented here. We thank the donors who have generously given, and continue to give, their objects for inclusion in our permanent collection, as well as the historians who have also graciously given their time and efforts over the years to provide us with first-rate essays and historic documentation for our many exhibition catalogs. Those important objects in our collection and those significant writings serve, in a sense, as the basis for this book. As with most of our previous books, this example is a publication of the Ernest R. Graham Study Center for Architectural Drawings at the Art Institute of Chicago.

More recently, specific people have helped us to realize this current publication, and they deserve our gratitude. In 2002 researchers Danielle Butler, Erin Komray, and Sonja Ostendorf assisted in the compilation of photographs published here and in gathering information on contemporary architects. This photographic research was completed by Annie Feldmeier in the Art Institute's Publications Department, in cooperation with Kate Butterly, our department's Collections Manager, and the Imaging staff of the Art Institute. Stanley Tigerman, an architect who has been central to the architectural scene in Chicago over the past three decades as well as an active participant on our own Advisory Committee on Architecture for more than twenty years, generously agreed to write the preface. Within the Publications Department, Associate Directors Robert V. Sharp and Amanda W. Freymann both added their years of expertise in editing and production, respectively, to the creation of this volume. Finally, David Morton of Rizzoli and the staff there all helped to shape this book into what we feel is an important landmark in itself to documenting architecture in Chicago, and our museum's role in this process.

JOHN ZUKOWSKY

The John H. Bryan Curator of Architecture
The Art Institute of Chicago

MARTHA THORNE

Associate Curator of Architecture
The Art Institute of Chicago

A

Abraham Lincoln Oasis, 134–135
Adler, David, 88–89, 98–99
Adler and Sullivan, 44–45
Adler Planetarium and Astronomical
    Museum, 198–199
Alschuler, Alfred S., 68–71
American Institute of Architects (AIA),
    19, 220, 221
American Medical Association (AMA),
    176–177
Ando, Tadao, 190–193
Antunovich Associates, 36
Architecture and Design Society, 15
The Architecture of Bruce Goff, 19, 22
Art Institute of Chicago Architecture
    Department
    Committee on Architecture 2003, 236
    Design Initiative Center, 225
    digital design data study, 231
    exhibitions, 12, 16–27, 144,
        148–149, 235–236
    history, 8–9, 12–26
    mission, 230
    oral history project, 13
    proposed addition, 225
    publications, 15–16
Attic Club, 88–89
Atwood, Charles, 36, 38–39
Avery Coonley Playhouse, 58–59

B

Becker, Lynn, 220
Beeby, Thomas, 19, 219
Bell, Robert E., 130
Bennett, Edward H., 52–55,
    78, 92, 97, 218
Bennett, Parsons, Thomas & Frost, 78–79
Bertrand Goldberg Associates, 124–125
Bilbao: Transformation of a City, 19
Blue Cross/Blue Shield of Illinois, 196–197
Blum, Betty, 13
Boeing Company, 174
Bonner, Darcy, 19
Booth, Laurence, 24, 26, 27, 219
Booth Hansen Associates, 208–209
Boulevard Apartments, 76–77
Brand, Jennifer, 15
Bridge Over Caldwell Avenue, 106–107
Brininstool & Lynch, 230, 231
Brook Architects, 230
Brownson, Jacques, 126
Brubaker, Charles William, 136

Buckingham, Kate, 78
Buckingham Fountain, 2–3, 78–79
Budilovsky, Michael, 162
Building for Air Travel (1996), 23, 24, 25
Burcher, John S., 172–173
Burgee, John, 168–169
Burlington Zephyr, 91
Burnes, Al, 120
Burnham, Daniel, Jr., 82–83
Burnham, Daniel H., 30, 31,
    32, 52–55, 218. *see also* D. H.
    Burnham and Company
Burnham, Hubert, 82–83, 92, 97
Burnham and Root, 31, 32–35, 36–37
Burnham Brothers, 82–83
Butterly, Kate, 15

C

Caldwell Avenue, bridge over, *see* Bridge
    over Caldwell Avenue
Carbide and Carbon Building, 82–83
Carson Pirie Scott, 1, 46–47
Carter, Drake & Wight, 30, 31
Century of Progress Exposition, 90–97
Cessna 337 Float Plane, 13
C.F. Murphy Associates, 118, 120–121,
    126–129, 136–139, 142–143,
    154–158, 198. *see also* Murphy/Jahn
Chatten, Melvin C., 85
Chicago and Northwestern Terminal
    Building, 162–163
Chicago Architectural Club, 140, 144
Chicago Architecture: 1872–1922, 16, 17, 18
*Chicago Architecture and Design:
    1923–1993*, 16, 19, 20, 21
Chicago Architecture Club, 220
Chicago Architecture Foundation, 11
Chicago Board of Trade, 154–155
Chicago Civic Center, 126–129
Chicago Municipal Pier (Navy Pier), 60–61
Chicago Seven, 144, 219–220
Chicago Stock Exchange, Trading Room,
    44–45
Chicago Tribune Tower, 64–67
Childs, David, 24
Childs & Smith, 100–101
Chinese American Service Center, 216–217
Claggett, Leonard, 172–173
Cohen, Stuart, 219
Congress Street Expressway, 106–107
Cranbrook Academy of Arts, 130
Crate and Barrel Headquarters, Inc.,
    178–179
Crate and Barrel Store, 178
Cret, Paul, 97

D

D. H. Burnham and Company,
    37, 38–43, 50–51, 82
David Adler, Architect (2002), 24, 27
David Haid & Associates, 134–135
DeStafano Keating Partners, 220
Dinkelberg, Frederick P., 50
Dubin, Henry, 77

Dubin and Eisenberg, 77
Dymaxion car, 90, 91

E

860–880 Lake Shore Drive, 112–115
Eisenman, Peter, 222
Elkins, Frances, 98
Epstein & Sons, 220
Ernest R. Graham Study Center for
    Architectural Drawings, 15
Exhibition Pavilion, 38, 39
exhibitions, 12, 16–26, 144, 148–149,
    235–236

F

Fellger Park, 230, 232–233
Ferriss, Hugh, 106
Field Building, 86–87, 88
Field Museum, 78
1500 Lake Shore Drive, 80–81
Fine Arts Building, 36–37
First National Bank Building, 136–137
Fisher Building, 40–43
500 West Erie, 221
Flatiron Building, 50–51
Ford, Ruth, 116
Forest Chapel, 12
Forster, Kurt, 22
Fort Dearborn, 69
Fragments of Chicago's Past, 15
Freed, James I., 219
Frost, Charles Sumner, 60
Fuller, R. Buckminster, 91
Fuller Building, 50–51

G

Gang, Jeanne, 24, 228, 230
Garofalo, Douglas, 24, 194–195, 225
Garofalo Architects, 194–195, 225, 228
Genther, Charles, 112, 134
Gladych, Stanley, 136
Goettsch, James, 156, 196, 221
Goff, Bruce, 19, 22, 116–117, 130
Goldberg, Bertrand, 124–125
Graham, Anderson, Probst & White,
    86–87, 88
Graham, Bruce J., 122, 140
Graham, Burnham and Company, 82
Graham, Ernest, 82
Greengard, B.C., 80
Greenwald, Herbert, 112
Greyhound/Trailways Bus Terminal,
    180–181
Griffin, Marion Mahony, 56–57
Griffin, Walter Burley, 56–57
Grimes, Ellen, 194–195
Grimshaw, Nicholas, 19
Grunsfeld, Ernest, 198
Guérin, Jules, 50, 51, 52, 53

H

Hadid, Zaha, 222
Haid, David, 134–135
Hammond, C. Herrick, 85

Hammond Beeby Rupert Ainge, 224
Hard Rock Hotel, 82
Harringer, Henry, 86
Harry Weese and Associates, 130–133
Hartray, Jack, 180
Head House, 62
Heitz, Gary, 22
Herbert A. Jacobs House, 104–105
Highways of the Future, 106
Hilberseimer, Ludwig, 108
Hilliard, David, 13
HNTB Architecture, 212–215
Holabird, John, 92, 97
Holabird and Roche, 72–75
Holcomb, F., 103
Holsman, Holsman, Klekamp & Taylor, 112
Horn, Gerald, 219
Hossack, George A., 81
Hotel Sofitel, 210–211, 221
Howells and Hood, 66–67
Hyde Park Arts Center, 225, 226–227, 228

I

Illinois Institute of Technology (IIT), 8,
    108–111, 144, 219, 220, 222–223
Illinois Regional Library for the Blind and
    Physically Handicapped, 146–147
Inland Steel Building, 122–123
International Terminal, 182–185

J

Jacobs, Herbert and Katherine,
    house, 104–105
Jacoby, Helmut, 139
Jahn, Helmut, 24, 143, 154–167, 219, 222
James R. Thompson Center (State
    of Illinois Center), 158–161
Janin, Fernand, 52
John Burgee Architects, 168–171
John Hancock Center, 140–141, 142
Johnson, Philip, 168
Johnson, Ralph, 174–175, 178–179,
    182–183, 221

K

Kahn, Fazlur, 140
Kaiser, William F., 118
Kamin, Blair, 220
Karl Friedrich Schinkel, 1781–1841,
    19, 22–23
Kathryn Quinn Architects, 230
Kennedy, Sheila, 223
Kennedy Violich Architects, 223, 225
Kersey Coats Reed House, 98–99
Koolhas, Rem, 15, 222
Krause Music Store, 45, 49
Krueck, Ronald, 19, 224
Krueck & Olsen Architects, 152–153
Krueck & Sexton, 223–224
Kurokawa, Kisho, 19

L

LaGrange, Lucien, 82, 221
Landon Bone Baker, 230

LaSalle National Bank, 86–87
Late Entries to the Chicago Tribune Tower Competition (1980), 148–149
Lautrup, Paul, 37
Legorreta & Legorreta Architects, 223
Lenox Building, 31
Lester B. Knight and Associates, 158
Lincoln Park House, 190–193
Lincoln Park Zoo Main Store and Rooftop Café, 200–203
Lipp, Franz, 12
Lippincott, Roy, 57
Little Village Academy, 186–189
Loebl Schlossman & Bennett, 126
Loebl Schlossman Bennett & Dart, 142–143
Lohan, Dirk, 198–199
Lohan Associates, 196–199
Lohan Caprile Goettsch, 221
London Guarantee and Accident Building, 68–71
Loos, Adolf, 148
Loyau, Marcel, 78

M

Mack, Jenny & Tyler Decorators, 74
Manny, Carter H., Jr., 136
Marina City, 124–125
Markow Residence, 194–195
Marzolf, Lee, 12
McClier Corporation, 15, 32, 220
McCormick Place, 138–139
McDonald's, 134, 150–151
McNally and Quinn, 80–81
McVickers Theatre, 45, 48
Merrill, John, 122
Messrs. Cluett Coon and Company, 38–39
Midway Airport, 212–215
Mies van der Rohe, Ludwig, 9, 11, 12, 108–115, 134, 138–139, 144, 152, 219
Millennium Park, 224
Mine, Richard Yoshijiro, 12, 64
Modern Trains and Splendid Stations (2002), 24, 26
Montgomery Ward Memorial Building, 100–101
Moore, Charles, 149
Moore-Ruble-Yudell, 149
Morgan, Charles, 77
Morton International Building, 174–175
Mumford, Luigi, 15
Murphy/Jahn Architects, 158–167

N

Nagle, James, 219
Nagle Hartray & Associates, 180–181
National Endowment for the Arts (NEA), 8, 13
National Endowment for the Humanities (NEH), 8, 15, 16, 19, 23, 24
Navy Pier, 60–61
NBC Corporate Center, 172

NBC Tower, 172–173
Netsch, Walter, 122
900–910 Lake Shore Drive, 112–113
North Avenue Beach House, 204–207
Northwestern Memorial Hospital, 100–103
North West Tower, 84–85

O

O'Hare International Airport, 23, 118–121, 82–85
190 South LaSalle Street, 168–171
One South Wacker Drive, 156–157
Owings, Nathaniel, 97, 122
OWPP, 220

P

PACE Associates, 112, 134
Painted Apartment, 152–153
Palmer House, 72–75
Pappageorge/Haymes Ltd., 40
Patrick Fitzgerald Architects, 230
Pattington Apartments, 77
Pelli, Cesar, 223, 224
Perkins, Chatten & Hammond, 84–85
Perkins, Dwight H., 85
Perkins, Lawrence, 136
Perkins & Will, 136–137, 174–175, 178–179, 182–183, 218, 220, 221
Piano, Renzo, 26, 225
Picasso, Pablo, 126
The Plan of Chicago 1909, 12, 52–55, 69, 78, 218
Portland Cement Company, 106
Prince, Bart, 19
Pritzker, Cindy and Jay, 13

Q

Quinn, James Edwin, 80–81, 106–107
Quinn, Kathryn, 19

R

Racine Art Museum, 230, 231
Ralph Burke Associates, 118–121
Reiss, Steven, 212–215
Reliance Building, 36, 39
Richard J. Daley Center, 126–127
Richard Ten Eyck Associates, 13
Rock Crest/Rock Glen, 56–57
Rock Valley College, 228–229, 230
Rogers, James Gamble, 100–101
Rookery Building, 32–35
Root, John Wellborn, 31
Ross Barney, Carol, 186
Ross Barney + Jankowski Architects, 186–189
Ruble, John, 147
Rudolph, Christopher, 19
Rummel, Charles, 136
Ruth Ford House, 116–117

S

Saarinen, Eero, 130
Saarinen, Eliel, 64, 130, 149

St. Patrick's Roman Catholic Church, 208–209
Saliga, Pauline, 8, 13, 15, 19
Schiff, Harold, 15
Schiff Foundation Fellowship, 15
Schlesinger and Mayer Store (Carson Pirie Scott), 1, 46–47
Schroeder, Ken, 219
Schweikher, Paul, 13
Sears Tower, 151, 218
Seijima, Kazuo, 222
Seventeenth Church of Christ Scientist, 132–133
Shaw, Alfred, 86
Shaw and Associates, 168, 176–177
SITE (Sculpture in the Environment, Inc.), 150–151
Skidmore, Louis, 97, 122
Skidmore, Owings & Merrill, 15, 24, 26, 97, 122–123, 126, 140–141, 142, 172–173, 220, 224
Skybridge, 221
Sky-Ride, 97
Slutsky, Rael, 164
Smith, Adrian, 15, 172–173
Smolka Wolff, Peggy, 140
Sobek, Werner, 222
Soldiers Club, 57
Solomon Cordwell Buenz & Associates, 178
Spaulding, Robert, 95
Spertus Institute of Jewish Studies, 223–224
Speyer, A. James, 12–13
Stanley Tigerman & Associates, 146–147
State of Illinois Center (James R. Thompson Center), 158–161
Stateway Gardens, 230
Stern, Robert A.M., 13, 148
Stewart-Bentley Building, 30
Studio Gang/O'Donnell, 216–217, 228, 230
Sullivan, Louis, 12, 44–49, 149
Summers, Gene, 138–139
A System of Architectural Ornament (Sullivan), 12, 45, 48

T

Takayama & Associates, 32
Tange, Kenzo, 176–177
Taylor, Marilyn, 24
Teng Associates, 210–211, 220
Thielbar and Fugard, 102–103
3400 North Sheridan Road, 62–63
Thomas, Cyrus W., 79
Thompson Ventulett Stainback & Associates, 139
Tigerman, Stanley, 15, 16, 19, 22, 24, 144–147, 219
Time-Life Building, 130–131
The Titanic, 144–145
Tower of Water and Light, 96–97
Trading Room of the Chicago Stock Exchange, 44–45

Travel and Transport Building, 91, 92–95
2400 North Lakeview Avenue, Painted Apartment, 152–153
2001: Building for Space Travel (2001), 23, 25

U

United Airlines, 91, 92
United Airlines Terminal One, 23, 164–167
University of Chicago, 223, 224
University of Illinois at Chicago, 220
Urban, Joseph, 97
Urbanworks, 230
USB Tower Lobby, 221

V

Valerio, Joe, 200–203
Valerio Dewalt Train, 200–203
Van Osdel, John, 68
Viguier, Jean-Paul, 210–211, 221
Vinci, John, 15, 58
Viñoly, Rafael, 223
VOA Associates, Inc., 60
Voorhees, Gmelin & Walker, 96–97

W

Walker, Ralph, 65, 97
Water Tower Place, 142–143
Weber, Peter J., 39, 40, 62–63
Weese, Ben, 219
Weese, Cynthia, 219
Weese, Harry, 130–133
Wenrich, John, 96
Wesley Memorial Hospital, 100, 102–103
Wetdesign, 142
Whang, Minkyu, 194–195
Wheeler, Daniel, 19, 24
Wheeler Kearns Architects, 204–207
White and Weber, 62
Whiteman, Maria, 19
Wierzbowski, Steven, 19
Wight, Peter B., 12, 30–31
Wilkinson Blender Architecture, 230, 232–33
Will, Philip, 136
William Worn Architects, 230
Wimberly Allison Tong & Goo, 142
Wines, James, 159
Winslow Brothers Company, 43
Wood, James N., 13
Woodruff, George, 81
World's Columbian Exposition, 36–39, 218
Wright, Frank Lloyd, 32, 58–59, 104–105, 219

Y

Yudell, Buzz, 147

Z

Zook, R. Harold, 65

PHOTOGRAPHY CREDITS

All photographs in this book are protected by the expressed copyright of the following individuals or institutions. Wherever possible photographs have been credited to the original photographers, regardless of the source of the photographs.

All photographs of works in the collection of The Art Institute of Chicago are © The Art Institute of Chicago and were produced by the Department of Imaging, Alan B. Newman, Executive Director.

Jacket front: Chicago Historical Society; photograph by Hedrich Blessing, HB-02137-A

Jacket back and spine: The Art Institute of Chicago

1: Courtesy of Hedrich Blessing, SN860C

2–3: © 1998 by Lawrence Okrent

5, 6, 7, 10–11, 12, 13, 22, 25, 26, 28–29, 30, 31, 33, 36–37, 38, 41, 44–45, 45, 46b, 48, 51, 53, 54–55, 56–57, 57, 59, 60, 63, 64, 65, 66, 70, 74, 74–75, 76–77, 79, 80, 81t, 82, 85, 86, 88, 90b, 94–95, 96, 97, 98b, 100, 103, 105b, 106, 107, 108, 109b, 111b, 112, 116b, 118–19, 123tr, 123br, 124, 128–29, 130, 133, 135b, 136, 138–39, 138b, 139b, 140, 143, 144–45, 146b, 148, 149, 151, 152, 154b, 156, 160, 162r, 164, 168, 170, 172, 174, 177 l, 178t, 180, 182t, 182b, 186-87, 187bl, 190, 195, 196r, 199b, 200, 204-05t, 204-05b, 208, 210b, 212t, 212b, 216, 217, 225b: The Art Institute of Chicago

8: Chicago Historical Society; photograph by William S. Engdahl for Hedrich Blessing, HB-18506-R4

14, 17, 18: © Van Inwegen Photography

20, 21: Courtesy of Stanley Tigerman; © 1993 Van Inwegen Photography

23: © 1994 Karant + Associates, Inc.; photograph by Barbara Karant

24: © Steinkamp/Ballogg Chicago; photograph by James Steinkamp

27, 81bl, 81br, 113: © Hedrich Blessing

32, 34, 35: Courtesy of McClier; photograph by Nick Merrick © Hedrich Blessing,

37: Photograph by C. D. Arnold © 1993 The Art Institute of Chicago

39: Ryerson & Burnham Archives, The Art Institute of Chicago; photograph by J.W. Taylor

40, 42t, 62, 67r, 77, 150: © 2003 Joel DeGrand Photography

42b, 43t, 43br: © PAPPAGEORGE/Haymes Ltd.

46t: Chicago Historical Society, ICHi-15065

47: Ryerson & Burnham Archives, The Art Institute of Chicago; photograph from the David Phillips collection

49: © Michael J. Pado

50: Ryerson & Burnham Archives, The Art Institute of Chicago; photograph by Detroit Publishing Co.

52: from Charles Moore, *Daniel H. Burnham, Architect: Planner of Cities* (Boston and New York: Houghton Mifflin, 1921).

58: Ryerson & Burnham Archives, The Art Institute of Chicago

61: Courtesy of Navy Pier

67 l: Photograph for the Chicago Tribune by Randy Belice © Chicago Tribune 2002

68, 69, 71, 221: Courtesy of Lohan Caprile Goettsch Architects; photograph by John Miller © Hedrich Blessing

72–73: Courtesy of the Palmer House Hilton

78: © 1998 by Lawrence Okrent

83: Ryerson & Burnham Archives, The Art Institute of Chicago; photograph by Chicago Architectural Photographing Co.

84, 114–15, 134: © John Zukowsky

87: Chicago Historical Society; © 1935 Hedrich Blessi ing, HB-01325-J

89: Courtesy of Hedrich Blessing; photograph by Steve Hall, P54936L

90t: Chicago Historical Society; photograph by Hedrich Blessing, HB-01823-F

91: Chicago Historical Society; photograph by Hedrich Blessing, HB-02781

93: Ryerson & Burnham Archives, The Art Institute of Chicago; from *A Century of Progress Photographs, 1933-1934: Photographs by Kaufman & Fabry*, gift copy presented to Potter Palmer

98t, 99, 176, 177r: Bob Harr © Hedrich Blessing

101: Ryerson & Burnham Archives, The Art Institute of Chicago; from *The American Architect* 131 (July 20, 1927)

102: Northwestern Memorial Hospital Archives, ca. 1960

104–05, 104: Ryerson & Burnham Archives, The Art Institute of Chicago; photograph by Jack Steinberg

109t: Chicago Historical Society; photograph by Hedrich Blessing, HB-15691-C

110: Chicago Historical Society; photograph by Bill Engdahl for Hedrich Blessing HB-18506-Z4

111t: Chicago Historical Society; photograph by Hedrich Blessing HB-18506-C4

116: Ryerson & Burnham Archives, The Art Institute of Chicago; photograph by Sidney K. Robinson

117: © John Gronkowski

118, 120–21: Courtesy of United Airlines

122: Photograph by Hedrich Blessing, 56446 D

123 l: Photograph by Hedrich Blessing, P45085C

125: Ryerson & Burnham Archives, The Art Institute of Chicago; photograph by Hedrich Blessing, Chicago Historical Society, HB-23215-H5

126: Chicago Historical Society; photograph by Hedrich Blessing, HB-25252-H7

127: Chicago Historical Society; photograph by Hedrich Blessing, HB-25252-V3

131, 132: Courtesy of Gensler

135t: Chicago Historical Society; photograph by Hedrich Blessing, HB-31235

137: Courtesy of Perkins and Will; photograph by Hedrich Blessing

142: Courtesy of Loebl, Schlossman & Hackl

146t: Courtesy of Stanley Tigerman; HNK Architectural Photography, Inc.

147: Courtesy of Stanley Tigerman

153: Courtesy of Hedrich Blessing, P45677D

154t, 155, 157, 158–59, 161, 162 l, 163, 223: Courtesy of Murphy/Jahn

165, 166–67: Courtesy of Murphy/Jahn; photograph by Timothy Hursley

169, 171: Courtesy of the John Buck Company

173: Courtesy of Skidmore, Owings & Merrill LLP; photograph by Nick Wheeler © Hedrich Blessing

175: Courtesy of Perkins and Will; photograph by Nick Merrick © Hedrich Blessing

176: Bob Harr © Hedrich Blessing

178b: Steve Hall © Hedrich Blessing

179, 183, 184–85: Nick Merrick © Hedrich Blessing

181: Courtesy of Nagle Hartray Danker Kagan McKay Architects

187bl, 188, 189: Courtesy of Ross Barney & Jankowski; photograph by Steve Hall © Hedrich Blessing

191 l, 191r, 192–93: Courtesy of Tadao Ando Architect & Associates; photograph by Shigeo Ogawa

194t, 194 b: © 1999 William Kildow

196 l, 197, 198, 199t: Courtesy of Lohan Caprile Goettsch Architects; photograph by Jim Steinkamp, Steinkamp-Ballogg

201, 202-03: Courtesy of Valerio Dewalt Train Associates; photograph by Barbara Karant, Karant + Associates, Inc.

205 br: Courtesy of Wheeler Kearns Architects; photograph by Lawrence Okrent 2000

206–07: Courtesy of Wheeler Kearns Architects; © Hedrich Blessing

209: Courtesy of Booth Hansen Associates; photograph by Nick Merrick © Hedrich Blessing

210t, 211: Courtesy of Sofitel Chicago, Accor Hotels and Resorts; photograph © Fabrice RAMBERT

213, 214, 215: Courtesy of HNTB; photograph by Scott McDonald © Hedrich Blessing, 2001

219: Courtesy Perkins and Will

224: Courtesy of Cesar Pelli & Associates, Design Architect; OWP&P Architect of Record

225t: Courtesy of Kennedy & Violich Architecture, Ltd.

226–27: Courtesy of Garofalo Architects

228: Courtesy of Studio Gang, photography by conflux

228–29: Courtesy of Studio Gang photography by Jeanne Gang

231: Courtesy of Brinistool + Lynch, LTD.

232-33: Courtesy of Wilkinson Blender Architecture, Inc.

234: Courtesy of Studio Gang